BARNES & NOBLE
BUSINESS BASICS™

take charge
of your career

by Cynthia Ingols and Mary Shapiro

BARNES
& NOBLE
BOOKS
NEW YORK

Barnes & Noble Publishing, Inc.
122 Fifth Avenue
New York, NY 10011

introduction

You can feel it—it's time for a change. Maybe you have a difficult boss who is stifling your progress, or perhaps your company just got bought out and you suspect lay-offs are coming. Maybe you want to explore a job that offers you more flexibility. Whatever the reason, you know your career needs help. What should you do?

Here's what career experts Cynthia Ingols and Mary Shapiro advise: "The old ways of looking at your career as something that happens to you are gone. To be successful these days, you need to manage your career as if it were a business. That means being proactive. You need to constantly keep on eye on what's happening in the market-place. Don't wait for the change to come to you—go after it. Keep on top of your strengths and work on your weaknesses; master the unwritten rules of corporate culture; manage your bosses and colleagues with finesse. And most important of all, know when to move up in your company and when to leave for a better position."

The good news is that the knowledge and skills you need to manage your career are right here in **Barnes & Noble Business Basics** *Take Charge of Your Career.* In it you will find smart advice on how to determine if your company is competitive or not (page 156); why you need to create and maintain a network (page 124); how to deal with recruiters (page 160); when and how to talk to your boss about a promotion (page 140); and who can help you design the right career path (page 24). It's all here—so get started today on creating your personal road map to career success.

Barb Chintz
Editorial Director, the **Barnes & Noble Business Basics**™ series

table of contents

Chapter 1 New rules for the new world
Managing your career 8   Ongoing career development 10
Your career portfolio 12   Setting goals 14   Skills 101 16
Getting specialized 18   The role of technology skills 20   Forces
shaping your career 22   Working with coaches 24   Building
ties with HR 26   Informal support 28   Now what do I do? 30

Chapter 2 Navigating corporate culture and diversity
Understanding corporate culture 34   Addressing diversity 36
Diversity drives the marketplace 38   Cross-cultural concerns 40
When multiple cultures collide 42   The issue of fit 44   Sexual
politics 46   Dealing with discrimination 48   Physical
challenges 50   Now what do I do? 52

Chapter 3 Working with your boss
Getting to know your boss 56   Managing the boss 58 Get in
the boss's head 60   Earn a gold star 62   Common types of
problem bosses 64   When you have a difficult boss 66   Be your
own PR agent 68   Use your reviews 70   Now what do I do? 72

Chapter 4 Managing your colleagues
Office politics 76   Types of politics 78   Problem colleagues 80
Feedback 82   Pulling your weight 84   Handling differences 86
The art of negotiating 88   Disagree with diplomacy 90
Conflict management 92   Now what do I do? 94

Chapter 5 Overturning career roadblocks
Figuring out what went wrong 98   Classic career mistakes 100
Owning up to mistakes 102   Communication blunders 104
Poor writing 106   E-mail snafus 108   The imperative to
change 110   Now what do I do? 112

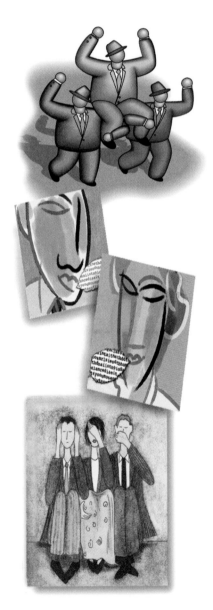

Chapter 6 Building strategic relationships
The importance of allies 116   Formal mentors 118   Group mentoring 120   Productive working relationships 122 Assessing your network 124   Professional associations 126 Nurturing your network 128   Now what do I do? 130

Chapter 7 Moving up
Internal opportunities 134   Getting project work 136   Getting a raise 138   Asking for a promotion 140   Negotiating for yourself 142   Interviewing in another department 144   Gendered expectations 146   Weighing a promotion 148   Now what do I do? 150

Chapter 8 Moving on: new job, new company
Focus on your future 154   How healthy is my company? 156 Looking ahead 158   When a recruiter calls 160   Analyze your future employer 162   Reviving a stalled career 164   Choosing to leave 166   Changing careers 168   Saying good-bye 170 Smooth exits 172   Now what do I do? 174

Chapter 9 Finding your balance
The right mix for you 178   Balancing work and life 180 Alternative career paths 182   Short-term challenges 184 Making big changes 186   Telecommuting 188   Taking early retirement 190   Now what do I do? 192

Glossary 194

Index 202

Authors 208

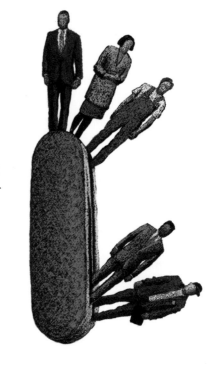

New rules for the new world

Managing your career 8
It's in your hands

Ongoing career development 10
The goal is to keep growing

Your career portfolio 12
Document your successes

Setting goals 14
Keep yourself on track

Skills 101 16
Bone up on your know-how

Getting specialized 18
Set yourself apart from the crowd

The role of technology skills 20
Stay on the cutting edge

Forces shaping your career 22
Top three big market changes

Working with coaches 24
Benefit from their expertise

Building ties with HR 26
The gatekeepers of your career

Informal support 28
Your personal board of directors

Now what do I do? 30
Answers to common questions

managing your career

The arc of your career

In the not-too-distant past, your career was something that happened to you. Very few people actively managed their career; rather, they waited for bosses to notice their work and promote them on to bigger and better things. Those days are gone. You are in charge of your career, not your boss or some long-outdated **old boy's network**. Moreover, people no longer typically advance in a straight line up through management in one company. More likely you will make a lateral move into a new project team or into a new area of the company—or even more likely you will move up by

joining a new company. In fact, research shows that most people change careers three to seven times in their lifetime.

Given this new reality, what should your career look like? What kind of career trajectory do most professionals in your field have now?

How do you find out about the stages of career development in your industry or company? Ask! As early as the job interview, you should feel free to ask about the typical career trajectory for the position you are seeking. This should also be a standard question to ask your boss during performance reviews.

The changing definition of "career"

Most likely your professional career will involve changing companies and functions as you explore new opportunities or interests, or seek to develop new skills. At times you will be working 60-hour workweeks; at other times you may work only 10 hours or less per week (due to your changing life priorities or an organization's changing staffing levels). As part of the new definition of "career":

■ The responsibility to optimize your career is clearly in your hands now.

■ There are multiple, equally valid **career paths** that you can choose over your lifetime in response to changes in the workplace and in your home life.

■ Your career path should reflect your own efforts to meet your goals and acquire your desired rewards and expectations—not others' ideas.

The basic questions

How often were you asked what you wanted to be when you were growing up? Lucky were the few who could definitively answer "doctor" or "teacher." This question is difficult enough to answer when you're a child, but in today's increasing complex world it's even harder. You can't just answer this question once, make a career decision, and assume your life course is all set. What will happen when you have a child, or get laid off, or when your partner gets a fabulous job offer 2,000 miles away? These answers will change over time, and so will your career response.

Although the ground may shift under your feet, being able to answer these basic questions about yourself will help you plot out a successful career path:

■ What do I enjoy doing? What do I get excited about? What makes me jump out of bed in the morning?

■ What am I good at? What are my skills and strengths?

■ What is important to me in my work? What do I want to accomplish? What will make me feel satisfied in my job?

ongoing career development

Committing to constant growth

Are you feeling "stuck" in your career or nervous about making a new job choice? Before you do anything, consider that creating a development plan for building your skills or knowledge isn't just a one-time thing: It means permanently changing how you think about career growth and how you go about achieving it. Committing to ongoing career development as a way of life and not just a quick fix is a lot easier if you make these three promises to yourself:

I will invest in lifelong learning You cannot let your knowledge go stagnant. More important, you cannot let your ability to learn go stagnant. **Lifelong learning** means revisiting your situation regularly, finding the new knowledge gaps, and bridging them with additional training. Getting an education is a continuous process—not just getting a degree.

I will develop self-awareness Self-awareness is the ability to see yourself accurately and to also be aware of how others see you. If you think others' perceptions are not accurate, then you need to find ways to correct them, or it can hold you back in your job. Self-awareness also means being honest with yourself about your talents and potential and setting realistic goals. Being self-aware also means paying close attention to the corporate culture of your current job (see chapter 2).

I will create a network of supportive colleagues and mentors Even CEOs need advisers to help them avoid unexpected career pitfalls. In the same way, you too need to develop a **network** of ongoing relationships with colleagues and **mentors** you can trust and who show an interest in helping you maximize your career. Such people can give you sound advice, warn you of career dangers, and spot opportunities for you. Remember, however, that these relationships need to be reciprocal, or such supporters may grow tired of your self-absorption and drift away.

New rules for career development

Learn another language Ideally, it should be one of the languages of the fastest-growing markets, such as Spanish or Chinese. Connect your language learning with some aspect of your career.

Be flexible While it is important to make plans, it is also a world that can turn plans upside down (witness the dot-com boom and bust). Create career development plans for the coming 18 months and then be flexible when new opportunities arise.

Build your résumé on value-adding projects Much work in the new world of work will be project-based. Learn how to work in project teams, how to lead them, and how to monitor and record the value that you added, created, or contributed. You will find how to do this on page 136.

Be a change agent Every organization needs people who know how to improve processes and bring about change. Start small and put those activities on your resume.

Be a technowizard Keep abreast of new technologies and learn how they are impacting your job and the marketplace.

Be a trend-watcher In the old days of the late 1990s, computer folks were getting high salaries and bonuses. Then jobs started going overseas and high-tech types stood in line at unemployment offices. Watch the trends and know what is going on.

Get international experience The globalization of the economy and the interconnection of the political and social environment calls for leaders who know and understand other cultures.

your career portfolio

Tracking the highlights
of your career for
easy access

If you are like most working professionals, you keep careful track of your work and your company's goals. If you are in sales, you keep track of new leads, note all sales, and keep on top of your quota goals; if you are in marketing, you track new product cycles; if you are in research and development, you track trends. But few career professionals actually take the time to document the progress of their careers. While some may collect their performance reviews, few actually have the documents that support their many career highlights. Nor do they have any notes on how they managed to think through tough decisions. You can start to take your career in hand by starting to document your progress. All that is required is an organizer and a notebook.

In the organizer, start compiling copies of e-mails or reports that show how well you handled a problem on the job. You are looking for those key pieces of paper that document how you managed things. Inside this organizer you can also keep copies of your performance reviews. The reason for this documentation is simple: It lets you see patterns in how you deal with job challenges.

Second, get a notebook. Consider it your career diary. In it you are going to start keeping tabs on your career goals, areas in yourself that you need to develop, and a host of other things. This is a private notebook, so keep it and your portfolio in a secure place at work—or at home, if you prefer.

The first thing to write in your career notebook is your **vision statement**. This should be just three or four lines describing your career aspirations, much like the mission statement a company might use to outline its objectives and activities. For example:

Vision Statement

My vision is to move out of my individual contributor role into management. I will expand my leadership skills by hiring effective team members, by training team members on the job, and by rewarding people for their individual and team contributions.

Quarterly statements

In a corporation, quarterly statements are critical documents that show how the company has fared over the past three months. Those statements are then compared to the previous statements to see how well goals were met.

Why not adopt this quarterly benchmarking and do a personal review of your career every three months. Take an hour or so to go over your previous three months of work and note what you did and why, and what were the results.

setting goals

The best way to measure progress

The great baseball player Yogi Berra famously once said, "You've got to be very careful if you don't know where you're going, because you might not get there." In other words, without a goal or destination in mind, you'll never know if you've accomplished what you set out to do.

In terms of your career, there is probably no truism more important than this one: You have to set goals—both long- and short-term ones—or you may not ever fulfill your dreams.

The first step is asking yourself: What are my career dreams? If you haven't thought about this in a while, now's the time. Take out your career notebook and write down any dreams you've ever had for your career—no matter how crazy they may sound.

Now take a close look at what you wrote. Which are your "must have" dreams? "Must have" dreams are the ones that are essential to your definition of career success, happiness, and a sense of fulfillment.

Think long and hard about which of these "must haves" mean the most to you, put them in order of priority, and then consider how you can achieve them. Write about them in your career notebook, using as much detail as you can—the goal is to turn them from vague ideas into vivid, concrete goals.

Make sure to set a time frame for achieving your goals. Management guru Peter Drucker recommends setting goals you can accomplish in 18 months or less; longer-term goals tend not to be achieved because conditions—not to mention your dreams—can change over time.

Some sample 18-month goals might be: "Hone my negotiation skills by taking a negotiation course at XYZ College," or "Learn Spanish by buying language tapes and practicing four days per week at 20 to 30 minutes at a time, and visit Mexico next year."

Attaining your "must haves"

Setting goals is one thing, but actually reaching them is another matter. Try the following tips for making your career "must haves" happen:

Check your progress regularly Decide how and with whom you will assess your progress, such as with a friend or colleague at the beginning of each month. Or note in your calendar when and how you will hold yourself accountable.

Take action to eliminate barriers Sometimes your plan will reach an impasse, such as if you get a time-consuming new work assignment. Whatever the situation, identify the obstacles and then find ways to overcome them.

Change your methods of attaining your goals Your schedule can change over time, so be flexible in the methods you use to reach your goals. For instance, instead of learning to speak Italian by taking a night course, you can listen to language tapes while commuting instead.

Have a backup plan Create at least one backup plan—or even two or three—to obtain your "must haves" if your first plan fails.

Reward yourself and celebrate When you achieve another goal or complete another step, pat yourself on the back. Take yourself out to dinner or buy yourself flowers—whatever it takes. The goal is to have fun and praise yourself for a job well done!

skills 101

Filling in the gaps

Once you've set your goals, you have to think concretely about how you are going to achieve them. In many cases, achieving them means building some new skills. But which ones? Everyone is different, but in today's highly competitive employment marketplace, there are certain skills that are especially critical. These include:

Writing skills This means writing clear, coherent, and effective reports, and using quantifiable data to support your arguments.

Negotiation skills This means being able to articulate what you want and knowing the trade-offs you'll accept to get your priorities met. It also means understanding varying perspectives and devising win-win strategies to bridge conflicts (see page 88).

People/management skills You should be able to understand others' points of view, direct projects and teams effectively, manage your emotions, and negotiate office politics with finesse (see pages 76–77).

Computer literacy Basic computer skills are a must in this high-tech age. At a minimum, you should know your way around a computer desktop and be able to use word-processing software, a spreadsheet program, and e-mail.

Appreciation As the workplace becomes more diverse, it's important to be accepting of people from a variety of backgrounds, who may have different perspectives and values.

Public speaking This means being able to develop a public speech or statement that is persuasive and appealing, and that gets your points across clearly—then presenting it confidently in front of an audience.

Foreign language skills The number of nonnative English speakers in the U.S. is growing exponentially, so if you want to be able to count them among your clients or customers, you need to be able to speak their language.

Developing a specialty

According to many HR experts, a surefire way to ensure that you are employable and promotable is to **specialize**. This is the process of acquiring and using knowledge in one particular career area. An example of this is a doctor who first goes through general medical training before going on to become, say, a cardiologist.

If you haven't already specialized in your field, consider the pros and cons of specialization. An advantage of expertise is that when people need specific advice or answers to detailed questions, they will turn to you.

A disadvantage of specializing, however, is that you may disregard important developments in other areas of your field. For example, some of the most innovative developments happen where two fields overlap, such as between technology and biology. By being focused on a very small area of either field, you could miss the larger picture.

Developing an expertise takes careful planning. Talk to colleagues, read up on your field, and attend professional conferences to learn how experts think that your field will develop in the future.

Some examples of fast-growing specialties in traditional fields

Law
Environmental law
Intellectual property law
Patent law

Medicine
Gerontology
Physical therapy
Medical assistants

Technical support
Networking systems
Database development
Webmasters

Business
Internet marketing specialists
Market researchers

getting specialized

To maximize your career potential, you need to be able to recognize and take advantage of changes and trends in your industry. Like a surfer riding a wave, staying on top means knowing which way the current is moving. It also requires adaptability and flexibility to deal with sudden swells.

It also means knowing—and being able to wield—the skill, talent, or information most valued by leaders in your particular industry. This "coin of the realm" (the currency that buys respect and status in a particular industry) varies from field to field.

In the academic world, for instance, publishing articles and books is the field's most highly prized accomplishment, and the one most necessary to career success. In the corporate world, some people advance their careers by taking responsibility for the profit and loss of a unit and finding ways to make the unit grow.

Do you know what the coin of the realm is in your profession? If not, set up informational interviews with people who have gone far in your field and ask them to describe what they did to move their careers forward. Did they learn a new software program or leadership initiative that helped give them the necessary edge to succeed? Did they get this training on their own or did the company provide it? In short, find out what they did to get ahead and then find out how you can follow in those footsteps.

Four Steps to Building Skills

No matter which of the six fundamental skills you want to build, you can follow these steps for getting there:

1. Analyze the gap between your current skill level and the capabilities that you want to achieve. The best way to gauge your skill level is to ask for feedback from your boss and others with whom you work.

2. Commit to closing the gap and set a time frame for doing so. In general, 18 months of moderate study or practice should move you from one level of skill up to the next (from intermediate to advanced, for example).

3. Make a list of ways you can acquire the skills, such as classes, organizations, tutoring, books, etc. If, for example, you want to develop your public speaking skills, then you might take a course, join Toast Masters (**www.toastmasters.org**), or have someone coach you on public speaking, giving you pointers on developing a speech and feedback on delivering it.

4. Record your practice sessions and rate your skills as you go along. When you feel you've improved, practice your skills for others and get feedback.

Where do you turn?

When it's time to build your skills, there are several people you can turn to for tips and ideas on how to get started. These people include:

Your boss or colleagues Sit down with your boss or colleagues that have the skills you want to build, and ask them how they went about it. They may have some suggestions for you that you have never considered.

Your employer Find out if your employer offers any relevant internal or external training programs.

Your community Check out the educational resources programs offered in your community, such as evening classes, workshops, or part-time degree programs. If your employer does not cover this training expense, consider the costs before you sign up.

the role of technology skills

**More than just
word processing**

There's no doubt about it: Technology and the Internet have changed the face of the working world, enabling us to work smarter, faster, and over longer distances. Being able to integrate new technologies into your work and manage virtual relationships will have a huge impact on your career. To maximize the potential benefits, there are two main things you need to do:

Regularly update your tech skills This means engaging in structured, challenging, educational activities throughout your career to keep your tech skills current. This could require taking a course over the Internet, signing up for a community-college certification program, or teaching yourself via instructional books or CDs.

Become familiar with the new forms of interaction By 2005, experts estimate that 25 percent of the American workforce will **telecommute**, or work from home by connecting to their offices via the Internet. But even so, people and relationships will continue to remain vital to accomplishing important work. So it's important that you learn how to manage these virtual relationships— whether you're the telecommuter or managing one. This requires staying connected both virtually and in person, and setting and keeping guidelines for doing so, among other things.

Are you an early adopter or a snail?

Your relationship to technology is going to have a great impact on your career, so analyzing the way you approach it can reveal the kinds of actions you need to take to optimize this relationship.

There are two basic ways that people respond to technology. Which type are you?

Early adopters

These are folks who read about, anticipate, and buy the latest high-tech gizmos. If this is you, make your techno savvy work for you and your career by doing the following:

1. Let people in your organization know that you are a techie who is on top of the latest trends. Share your knowledge, especially with senior management who may not be as comfortable or familiar with new technologies.

2. Learn a specialty in addition to technology so that you build your workplace value and avoid becoming pigeonholed. If you are a tech expert and want to succeed in business, take business courses or get an MBA. Or if you are interested in money and finance, study economics/finance.

Snails

These are people who are anxious about change and slow to adopt high-tech innovations. If this describes you, then put the following strategies into action:

1. Talk to early adopters on a regular basis and ask what's new. When you have questions, get assistance from techies and watch what they do.

2. Push yourself to read an occasional article about technology trends and developments. Specialized tech Web sites such as **www.cnet.com** and **www.whatis.com** are great for product reviews and tech news.

3. Use the Help menu in your software. The Help sections can be incredibly useful, and most are easy to understand. You can also sometimes find free online tutorials for new software. And make sure to keep instruction manuals for new equipment within easy reach.

forces shaping your career

Changes in the market always mean changes in your career development

Thanks to the Internet, globalization, and changes in demographics, the world of business and the pace of business have changed dramatically. The forces at work on your career are huge:

Globalization There's a good chance that the car you drive was designed in Japan, built in California, and runs with gas from Saudi Arabia. Every aspect of American life, including your career, is affected by events around the world.

Demographics There have been huge shifts in populations in age and country of origin. When you were born determines how you fit into the demographic trends of the population at large. Demographics determine what products are growing and waning and how many people you're competing against for a job. Additionally, demographics are affected by a whole world full of consumers and job applicants.

Technology The integration of the Internet into the marketplace has drastically altered the way companies do business.

Because of these three market forces, the speed of doing business has gone from 9 to 5, five days a week, to 24/7. Thus, your bosses rarely have the time to look out for you. They're busy keeping their heads above water.

Outsourcing and you

Another growing workplace trend is **offshoring**, or **outsourcing**, which means sending manufacturing work, or work that can be digitized (translated into computer files or done via the Internet), to countries where labor is cheaper. What does this mean for you? This means that you may need to work harder to make yourself indispensable to your organization so that your job is not sent abroad. Specializing (see page 17) and building your skills are two ways to do that. But if you know your job is almost certainly going to be outsourced eventually, or outsourcing has already begun at your company, it may be time to look into careers that center around work that is hard to offshore; these are jobs that require hands-on work or face-to-face interaction, like healthcare, computer networking, counseling, and teaching.

Specific changes that are impacting jobs today

Aging of the baby boomers The huge, market-driving population of people born between 1946 and 1964, known as the baby boomers, is starting to retire. The career choices they made, the companies they started, and the market changes they brought about are all in flux now, thanks to younger generations that are starting to take over and make changes.

Women will be an even stronger force in the business world Over the past 30 years, there have been dramatic changes in women's participation in the U.S. labor force. In 1970, about 43 percent of adult women were in the labor force; by 2000, 61 percent of adult women worked and women comprised 47 percent of the labor force. Soon it is expected that women will make up more than 50 percent of the labor force.

Diversity In 1999, African-Americans were the largest minority in the United States, accounting for 12 percent of the population. About 11.5 percent of the population classified themselves as Hispanic. Approximately 4 percent were Asian or Pacific Islander and less than 1 percent were American Indians. And in 1999, 72 percent of the population was white. Hispanics are projected to outnumber African-Americans early in the 21st century. By 2025, it is estimated that Hispanics will be 18 percent of the population and African-Americans will be 13 percent. During the same time period, white Americans are expected to decline by 10 percent. What does this mean for your career? It means that you need to get savvy about diversity issues and how they can affect your career. For more on this, see pages 36–43.

working with coaches

A **coach** is exactly what it sounds like: someone who provides one-on-one guidance and instruction designed to improve your knowledge, skills, and work performance. Some companies offer training with coaches. If yours does not, then consider hiring a professional career coach who can help you identify your career path and create strategies to achieve your career goals.

Many corporations hire **executive coaches** for top-level personnel. Recognizing that leadership development requires individual attention, the trend is to hire coaches for middle managers too. The aim is to improve the performance of their managers in a specified area. The process usually has five steps:

- The coach learns about the trainee's job and current level of performance.
- The coach and trainee agree upon performance objectives.
- They come up with a plan, a schedule, and a deadline for meeting these objectives.
- The coach observes the trainee and gives feedback.
- The coach and trainee assess the level of improvement at the end of the coaching period and determine whether the objectives have been met; if not, a new coaching plan is created.

If your organization gives you a choice between coaching or a training program, weigh the pros and cons carefully. The advantage of coaching is that it's individualized and focused on you and your particular job. Plus, if you build a good relationship with your coach, that can translate into a vital and well-connected contact in your network. By contrast, training programs are group activities that can provide a wealth of strategic relationships, but may or may not satisfy your specific developmental requirements.

More and more corporations offer coaching these days, but if yours doesn't, you can always hire an independent career coach for yourself. To find one, ask knowledgeable colleagues for recommendations. Talk to them and compare their approaches. Choose one with whom you have good chemistry, and create a six-month work plan with goals.

Ask the Experts

Our department head is retiring next year, and since I'm designated to succeed him, he wants me to find an executive coach to train me to take over. How do I go about finding a good one?

Since executive coaches specialize, you will first want to decide on skills that you would like to develop or improve. Then, ask trusted colleagues to recommend some coaches. More than likely, a colleague or two will have already used a coach. If not, then check sites like the International Coach Federation (**www.coachfederation.org**). Once you have a short list of three of four coaches, interview them—preferably face-to-face. Ask about their style of working and assess the chemistry between you. If you are careful in your selection process, you will likely be able to establish a strong working relationship that will help ease your transition into the role of department head. Plus, the coach may become an important and trusted contact in your network.

My company offers a coaching program to its middle managers. We received a list of coaches to choose from, and I've been working with the one I chose for six months now, but I don't feel as if her coaching is useful. What should I do?

The first thing to do is to have a conversation with your coach about what is and is not working for you. Somehow there is a misalignment between your expectations and what is happening in your sessions. When you have your conversation with your coach, be as specific as you can be. Give examples of what is and is not working. Decide on practical goals and how you will measure when you reach them. Then go through three more sessions, using the new format upon which you two agreed. If you are still dissatisfied, inform HR; it's possible that your coach is ineffective with others too and that someone in HR will know that and will help you pick a new one. Or it is possible that you are not well matched. In that case, it would be smart to have HR help you end the coaching relationship and find a new coach.

building ties with HR

Many employees overlook the importance of getting to know people in their HR departments, figuring, "I already have a job, so why do I need them?" But HR is really the backbone of an organization. It recruits, trains, and rewards an organization's most important asset: its people.

To get yourself in on this circuit, you need to form solid relationships with HR. This department holds the keys that can open the door to your next great job or project, and its three main responsibilities can greatly impact your career:

Recruitment HR folks know the skill sets and attributes that managers are seeking in their hires. Knowing what skill sets are vital to your company can help guide your career effectively.

Training and development programs HR people have inside knowledge about new training programs, quotas, and the advantages of various training courses. Plus, they often help nominate employees for prestigious training programs and match mentors and mentees. In short, they have the inside info and perspective and are involved in processes that can benefit your career.

Reward systems Most HR departments have **compensation specialists**, experts in pay systems and bonuses, and **benefits specialists**, who deal with health insurance and 401(k) programs. While they will not divulge specific or confidential information, they can help you understand these systems in general so you can negotiate for better compensation and benefits down the line.

So now that you know why you need connect with HR, how do you do it?

1. Regularly share your career goals with the appropriate HR employees. Go out to lunch or stay in touch by phone or e-mail.

2. Build reciprocity into this relationship. Send them interesting articles, point them toward well-qualified internal and external job candidates, and offer to help mentor or train new employees.

FIRST PERSON SUCCESS STORY

Borrowing from a smart HR recruiter

A close colleague of mine works in HR at our company and she is amazing at her job. What impresses me is how current she is on all the changes in the marketplace. I finally sat down with her and asked her what her secret was. She told me that every time someone was newly hired at the company, she took him to lunch or dinner. Then she would purposefully ask questions about career topics. These informal conversations provided her with inside information on what was going on regarding work trends at competing firms. I decided to use the same tactic. Every new hire I make, I take out to lunch and then "interview" him about his thoughts on the work world and changes in trends. I have learned so much from these lunches and have also helped make new team members feel welcome.

—Sarah M., San Diego, CA

informal support

Gathering informal
information, advice,
and wisdom

Informal career networks can be just as valuable as formal ones like professional associations. To tap informally into the wisdom of others and put your career on the fast track, management expert Tom Peters suggests forming your own **personal board of directors**: a group of people dedicated to your success. Here are three ways to set up your own kitchen cabinet:

The hobby club Here you find a group of like-minded professionals who share the same hobby, be it gourmet cooking or birdwatching. Your goal is to arrange a social gathering around this hobby. Once you have formed friendships, it is easy to steer the conversation toward work-related issues.

The alumni group Former schoolmates can be a great source of information. Why not e-mail those alumnae who live nearby and work in the same industry as you do and suggest setting up informal gatherings six times a year? You can meet at someone's house or a restaurant. The idea is to have a social meeting where you can share stories about school days as well as information about jobs and industry trends and opportunities.

Affinity groups Sometimes it is easier to meet informally when you share an affiliation, such as race, gender or religion. Informal women's networking groups, for instance, have proven very successful in helping career women keep on track.

Former colleagues Good work relationships can last a lifetime. Be sure to keep up contacts with former colleagues. They can be extremely helpful when you need a sounding board. Be sure to make yourself available to them when they need feedback.

FIRST PERSON SUCCESS STORY

The power of a like-minded group

Almost 20 years ago, I was working for a prestigious boutique consulting firm run by a high-powered husband-and-wife team. They were the stars and I was the workhorse. To grow the business, I did everything from negotiating contracts and making travel arrangements to buying office supplies. After 10 years in the same position, I realized that, while the pay was good, I was not developing professionally. I knew that I wanted to leave, but I didn't know what I wanted to do next.

A friend told me that several women my age who were also feeling stuck in their careers were starting a career support group. Six women, including me, came from wildly different business and academic backgrounds and met once a month for approximately two years. At each meeting, we socialized for a limited time, then got down to business: examining our professional lives through the eyes and ears of others who were committed to our development. This informal support group pushed me to define my strengths and clarify my vision of my next job. Plus, the monthly check-ins held me accountable for engaging in important tasks, such as going on informational interviews. I also found comfort in listening to the stories of others who were struggling with similar issues.

Eventually, I felt brave enough to make some major decisions: I quit the firm, took some training courses, and followed my childhood dream of becoming a travel agent. I now own my own travel agency, and to this day I still stay in touch with the group. I will always be grateful to them for helping me through that difficult time.

—Andrea P., St. Paul, MN

now what do I do?

I've been working in customer support for five years at a large corporation, and recently I heard rumors that they're going to move 80 percent of our jobs to India next year. Is there any way I can make myself indispensable so that I won't be laid off?

Work that is outsourced, or offshored to other countries, tends to be routine rather than highly creative work focused on problem-solving. To protect yourself, you might deepen your knowledge of a difficult-to-service product. In other words, make yourself a specialist in a customer support area that is considered nonroutine and not easy to outsource. Alternatively, position yourself as a particularly creative problem-solver. If neither of these options matches your skill set, then now—not after you're laid off—is the time to consider a new career in a field that requires hands-on or face-to-face work (such as the trades or medical care). Investigate possibilities and get the training you need. You will weather this trend much better if you prepare ahead of other people in your position.

I have had three jobs in two years in the financial services industry. Each time, I've been laid off when my department has been computerized. Help! How do I find stable work?

Since many organizations are downsizing and saving money by going high-tech in this hypercompetitive environment, your stability will need to come from within yourself. First, take heart: You've done a very good job of consistently finding work in your field. This suggests that you have a solid knowledge of the industry, which can only benefit your career. In addition to industry knowledge, however, it sounds like you need to make yourself a more valuable player—one that can't be phased out by a computer. How? Pick up some new skills. Here's a three-step process:
1. Assess your current skills. Which ones haven't been upgraded in a while? How solid is your IT knowledge?
2. Decide on the skills you want to develop over the next 18 months.
3. Get the education or on-the-job training you need to reach your 18-month goals.

My twins, Amy and Josh, are graduating from college soon, and they're not sure what they want to do for a career. What advice can I give them?

First, emphasize to them how important it is to follow their dreams and find a career that they love. Then encourage them to talk to their college counselor about taking diagnostic inventories (standardized personality tests like Myers-Briggs, aptitude or skills tests, or interest inventories) that can reveal the kinds of careers they are best suited for.

You might also want to suggest they research future job trends. At the moment, aging baby boomers are creating a rising demand for home healthcare, nursing, and geriatric services.

In addition, as the U.S. population grows more diverse, there will be more opportunities for people with language skills. For example, by 2025, Hispanics will make up 18 percent of the population. Those who speak Spanish will be well positioned to provide services for this growing demographic group.

Helpful Resources

WEB SITES

CareerPlanner.com
www.careerplanner.com
Take advantage of online career tests, one-on-one career counseling sessions with leading headhunters and recruiters, and free career planning information, advice, and ideas.

The Job Hunter's Bible
www.jobhuntersbible.com
Info and links to a number of inventories, as well as job-hunting and career advice from Richard Boles, author of the classic career planning guide, *What Color Is Your Parachute?*

WetFeet.Com
www.wetfeet.com
Info on employers and tips from industry experts that prepare you for the job search.

BOOKS

The Practical Coach: Management Skills for Everyday Life
by Paula J. Caproni

Career Warfare: 10 Rules for Building a Successful Personal Brand and Fighting to Keep It
by David D'Alessandro

Trendspotting: Think Forward, Get Ahead, and Cash in on the Future
by Richard Laermer

Global Trends 2005: An Owner's Manual for the Next Decade
by Michael J. Mazarr

Navigating corporate culture and diversity

Understanding corporate culture 34
The secret language of your workplace

Addressing diversity 36
Diversity is in the eye of the beholder

Diversity drives the marketplace 38
Accessing diverse populations

Cross-cultural concerns 40
It's a small world, after all

When multiple cultures collide 42
Negotiating your diverse identities

The issue of fit 44
Playing by their rules

Sexual politics 46
Keep the bedroom out of the boardroom

Dealing with discrimination 48
Be aware of what's legal and what's not

Physical challenges 50
When you need special support

Now what do I do? 52
Answers to common questions

understanding corporate culture

The rules of the wild

Your career success is directly linked to your understanding of corporate culture. What's the culture like at your company? The best way to find out is to look at the **norms**—both the implicit and explicit rules for behavior. They guide what people do so that their behaviors uphold the community's underlying values. For example, at one organization, it may be perfectly acceptable for you to stop by the boss's office and ask a question, while at another, you'd get yelled at if you did this. Likewise, getting the work done may be what matters most at one company, while at another, what counts is being at your desk for 10 hours each day.

Norms can include guidelines for everything from how to behave in meetings to who should fix paper jams in the photocopier. To get ahead, you need to play by these rules so that you'll be seen as respectful, productive, and committed. The good news is that if you do follow these rules, you will also be valued and rewarded. Don't play by these rules (either knowingly—or worse, unknowingly) and you'll suffer the consequences.

Just like a tourist who doesn't follow local customs, you may be seen as rude and disrespectful if you don't abide by your organization's norms. The easiest path to success in an organization is to know the rules and follow them. Or to leave if those norms don't mesh with your personal goals.

To find out what the norms are at your workplace, plug into the company grapevine. Keep yourself abreast of shifts in company culture by having lunch with coworkers and attending company social functions. Arrive at meetings a few minutes early to chitchat. Volunteer for interdepartmental committees so you can learn what's happening outside of your department. Keep your ear to the ground, and eventually you'll learn the rules.

Figuring out the norms

How well do you know the rules of your organization? And are they rules you can live with? Analyze your organization's approach in these major areas:

What information is shared and how:
- Is it done verbally or mostly in writing? On a "need to know" or FYI basis?
- Does it always follow a strict chain of command?
- Is it only shared when it's bad news?
- Hoarded and used for power or shared equally?

How time is used:
- What is the expected workday: 9 to 5? 8 to 8?
- Is the number of hours worked more important to the company than the actual work completed?
- How quickly are you expected to respond to e-mails?
- Is commitment only determined by spending long hours at work?

How decisions are made:
- Does the boss make decisions or is it done by consensus?
- Are decisions based on intuition or data?
- What gets rewarded? Taking risks? Not failing? Maintaining the status quo?
- Do major decisions get made on the golf course or in other informal arenas?

How conflict is handled:
- Is blame immediately assigned to a person or group?
- Is there an effort to learn from past mistakes?
- Can people disagree publicly or only in private?

The role of social interaction:
- Do people socialize first and then get "down to business"?
- Do they address each other by first names?
- Do they talk business in the hallway or only at scheduled meetings?

How relationships are structured:
- Can you talk to any senior person or only your boss?
- Who sits where in meetings?

addressing diversity

Understand how you are like— and not like— your coworkers

Take a look around your workplace. Even if it seems like everyone has about the same level of education or roughly the same income level, your colleagues really do come from all walks of life. In your department, you may work with an African-American, two colleagues from India, one white female from the American South, one Japanese-American who just graduated from college, and your soon-to-retire boss. Talk about diversity!

Many people confuse diversity with minority status. But diversity goes beyond the minority issues of gender, race, or religion. That's because it looks at traits and characteristics of people (called **social identities**), such as age, disability, education, family status, learning styles, military service, sexual orientation, even life experiences. In other words, we all share certain affinities with one another. And corporations have now learned that it is these affinities that inform many of the decisions people make—from their choice of career to the car they want to buy.

Because diversity is one of the leading market forces, it is now critical to the success of companies, and they have implemented a number of programs to help everyone feel a part of one team. Many companies now have mentoring programs, and networking groups. Moreover, senior management is judged on how well they foster diversity. That's why, as you plan out your career, you need to pay close attention to diversity issues. That means figuring out if you have any hidden—or not so—stereotypical expectations for any of the various affinity groups in your workplace.

Is your company diverse?

There are several ways to investigate just how "diversity friendly" your organization is without raising any red flags. Here are some areas to investigate:

■ **What kinds of people are at the top?** Go to your company's Web site and look at the list of their senior officers. Look at the organization chart or the personnel directory. Is there diversity in the surnames of management? Are there any women on the senior management committees?

■ **Who are the company's customers?** Often a company seeks to hire employees who reflect the demographics of their target market because they think these employees can lend insight into marketing and sales strategies. Is this the case in your company? If so, is this a diverse group?

■ **Observe the meeting dynamics.** The next time you go to a meeting, pay close attention to how it progresses. Do people of color or those with physical challenges play any major roles? How do the women interact with others? Are they front and center or do they take a more passive role?

■ **Check for the presence of "affinity groups" in your company.** These are groups of people with some common characteristics (whether race, gender, job function, or hobby) who come together to support one another or socialize. If there are no groups like this, that should tell you something.

■ **What kinds of positions are held by people like you?** If you belong to a minority group, try to get a feel for how many people like you are employed by your company and how high they are in the management hierarchy.

■ **Ask HR about your company's minority recruitment and retention programs.** Talk to HR to find out what kinds of minority training and recruitment programs your company supports, if any. Is there an established mentoring program? If so, does it provide specialized mentoring for minorities?

■ **Check out lists of "diversity friendly" companies.** Many business magazines and newspapers publish annual lists of the top 25 (or top 10) companies for African-Americans, women, or the physically challenged, based on their hiring, promotion, and retention practices. Is your company on the list?

diversity drives the marketplace

These days, smart companies are seeking more diverse personnel to help them stay in tune with a global economy. They want people from all backgrounds to feel comfortable coming up with new ideas for doing business that will help them tap into the ever-expanding, diverse markets in the U.S. and abroad. Diverse employees are the closest link that companies have to growing markets of diverse consumers. They can help create marketing plans that reach out to these populations in culturally sensitive and culturally knowledgeable ways, expanding the reach of a company's product.

To encourage this, many companies are offering special programs to support diverse employees, and grooming them for manage-

ment positions and for more visible roles in the company. Some corporate initiatives to support diversity include:

■ **Diversity awareness and support** To promote a "culture of inclusion," companies offer diversity training and some have executive diversity councils focused on the needs of diverse employees and customers. Others strive to include more diverse suppliers and vendors, and some support nonprofit aid programs for their diverse customers.

■ **Career development programs** To foster retention of diverse employees and to recruit new ones, many companies offer targeted management, leadership, and skill-building workshops. They are also including more diverse employees in **succession planning**.

■ **Mentoring** These supportive relationships, in which senior employees offer career advice and support to more junior ones, are especially useful for diverse employees, particularly when both mentor and mentee come from the same background.

■ **Affinity and networking groups** In these corporate-sponsored groups, colleagues united by gender, race, or even country of origin support and advise each other, building ties that can help them get ahead.

If you find yourself in a company that doesn't encourage or support diversity, consider finding a more diversity-friendly company that has the resources and "manager buy-in" to make diversity a top priority. You'll stand a better chance of climbing the corporate ladder faster.

FIRST PERSON　SUCCESS STORY

Putting your diversity to work

I decided to move my career forward by building experience on the marketing side of the business. I figured that the best way to do this was to get assigned to a high-visibility research project on making our company's software products more appealing to the Hispanic market. To get my name in the running, I talked with key people in product development, asked my boss to recommend me to the hiring manager, and asked the hiring manager to put me on the list of candidates. Then I did something creative that I was later told really made my candidacy stand out: I sent the search committee a fictitious press release announcing what a good choice I was.

It started out, "Ace Software, best known for its award-winning graphics packages, has assembled a dynamic team to research the Hispanic market. A key player is Mercedes Green, a young go-getter with a proven track record of success. With her ability to lead focus groups and draw out information from prospective customers, she'll be a true asset. When asked how her previous experience will be useful, Mercedes said, 'I grew up in a bicultural home and speak Spanish fluently. I can respectfully connect with our potential consumers and find out what they want. We can then use that information to build products that are attractive, useful, and profitable.'"

—Mercedes G., Houston, TX

cross-cultural concerns

When seeing eye-to-eye can be difficult

You work hard to expand your expertise. You come prepared to meetings, although you may not always get a chance to speak. You are quick to say "yes" when your boss asks you to do something, and then you do it well. If you run into problems, you try to fix them yourself. So why did you just get passed over for a promotion?

If you and your boss come from different cultural backgrounds, the two of you may be judging your performance by different standards. You each may be following your own culture's ideas about what professional, competent, and promotable behavior looks like. For example:

■ If you wait to be invited into a conversation during a meeting, your boss may see you as unprepared and unmotivated if interrupting is considered the standard way to enter a conversation in her culture.

■ If you deflect compliments about your work, constantly insisting that "it was nothing," your boss may see you as less competent if bragging about or even acknowledging accomplishments is considered acceptable in her culture.

■ If you downplay your concerns about a decision, your boss may see you as dishonest or uncertain if her culture calls for speaking directly and "telling it like it is."

You need to work at bridging the divide. And many times, if you make a wholehearted attempt to do so, people will meet you halfway. In other words, if you make it obvious that you are willing to learn and play by the rules of the dominant culture and/or your boss's culture, your boss will likely recognize your efforts and respond with greater cultural sensitivity.

The name game

No one wants the embarrassment of mispronouncing a name, and some—including employers—will avoid this possibility altogether by not interacting with someone who has an unfamiliar name. If yours is hard for English speakers to pronounce, give your colleagues a hand by putting a phonetic version of your name next to the nameplate on your desk and taking extra time to teach people how to pronounce it. When introducing yourself, slowly pronounce each syllable. Be patient and repeat it if necessary. You might also consider using an Anglicized version of your name or an English nickname for the workplace.

Fitting in

Be known for your talents—not your cultural identity. Make an effort to fit in. It is essential to being considered a team player and to getting the recognition you deserve. Fitting in means following the dominant culture's rules for behavior and dress. In most of corporate America, these rules include:

- Dressing conservatively in standard Western professional attire

- Using standard English (avoid cultural slang)

- Following Western grooming practices (neat hairstyles and trimmed facial hair, modest jewelry, proper footwear, etc.)

Fitting in doesn't mean giving up your own culture for good, but it does mean adopting the behavioral norms of the professional group you are associated with for now. Know when and where to follow your own cultural protocols in the workplace, and when not to.

when multiple cultures collide

Learning to balance two sets of norms

Imagine that in your company the way to show respect is to "tell it like it is," or to give the boss the bad news directly—without sugarcoating it. Those are the norms or how things are done based on your company's culture. The people in at the top of your company's hierarchy usually set these norms. If your social identity (defined by your race, gender, culture, and sexual orientation, among other things) matches theirs, you'll most likely feel comfortable following the same rules. But what if your social identity is different? Chances are the way some things are done at your company will seem strange to you at times.

How do you reconcile these two sets of norms? It's like trying to play soccer with multiple sets of rules. First you have to learn the prevailing set of rules. Then you need to decide which of those rules you can comfortably adapt to. In doing so, keep these things in mind:

■ Your work environment (and not the political or social environment) defines which social group is the majority and which is the minority in your company. For example, because most people in nursing are female, men form the "diverse" or minority group in this field. In some parts of the country where there are large Hispanic populations, Caucasians are considered "diverse" in the workplace.

■ You have multiple identities, some of which will come to the forefront during various work situations. For example, you may be a single Native-American woman, but you may identify most with your gender when you are working with all women, with your marital status when you are working with all single people, and so on. By switching within your multiple identities in each of these situations, you can find a common denominator with your colleagues.

Ask the  Experts

I've just graduated from college and am looking for a job in marketing. As an African-American, what kinds of companies should I be thinking about joining?

Smart companies seek out diversity. A company that employs many diverse people in management positions is usually one that supports and nurtures its diverse employees, helping them to get ahead. See page 37 for more on how to find diversity-friendly companies.

My boss told me that in our company mentoring program, you get to choose your mentor. I am an Asian-American woman. What kind of mentor should I choose? Should I seek out someone who comes a background similar to mine?

Don't limit yourself to mentors that match your social identity. Conversely, don't expect someone to want to mentor you just because you share a racial identity. Instead, choose a mentor who has similar values when it comes to work, life, goals, and rewards. For more on mentoring, see pages 118–119.

the issue of fit

Are you a trailblazer?

Think of your closest friend. Does she share your taste in music, your work ethic, or your passion for tennis? Chances are, you have at least a few things in common—that's why you're friends. In your personal life, you often choose to be with people who are somehow similar to you. You do the same in your professional life, but with much larger consequences.

A central career question is: How important is it to have a lot in common with the people in your workplace? Are you happier when your social identity is similar to those around you and you easily **fit** in? Or are you a **trailblazer**, working in a company where you are one of the few women, African-Americans, or gay people? There is no one "right" answer, but there is a right answer for you.

Trailblazing can be particularly challenging. You have to first learn the rules that the majority group plays by—rules that are often implicit and unspoken. Next, you have to follow rules that may be different from your own. If you perform well, everyone sees it, and this can be good for your career. But if you perform poorly, it may not only impact your career, but the careers of others in your identity group.

Knowing your own temperament can help you determine if you can handle the stresses of being a trailblazer. Key survival characteristics include:
- Feels at ease with uncertainty and ambiguity
- Achieves satisfaction from working alone
- Can get social and emotional needs met outside of work
- Skilled in conflict resolution and negotiation
- Confident and has a firm sense of personal worth
- Satisfied with internal praise rather than the praise from others
- Has solid coping skills and a strong network of support

Clearly, it's not easy being a trailblazer, but the rewards can be enormous. You can not only push your career forward—you can help pave the way for others like you.

Getting along

These days employers hire and promote people because they have the right skills and the motivation to do the job and because they understand the role of diversity in the workplace and the marketplace. As you build your career, you need to learn how to bridge many diversities Here are some tips:

- Clarify why you may go about your job differently than coworkers so there is less chance of misunderstanding. Ask questions and be direct. For example, if your coworkers keep their office doors open, and you need quiet to do your best thinking, explain this to your boss and ask if it's okay to shut your door for a few hours each day. Talking about differences openly and matter-of-factly reduces your risk of being seen as disrespectful or unfriendly.

- Look for common ground with coworkers, but don't assume there is some, just because you are both women, or both African-American, or both immigrants. Seek out common interests by sharing information about yourself. Finding common ground around children, sports teams, or hobbies is a powerful way of bridging differences.

- Create opportunities to interact with the majority group. People tend to gravitate toward others who are like them: Conversations flow smoothly, no one gets offended, and actions aren't misinterpreted. But if you don't make a point of reaching out to coworkers who are different from you, you may end up further isolating yourself from the majority group.

sexual politics

Keeping overtly sexual behavior out of the office

One aspect of the workplace that can create unwelcome tension between coworkers is sexual politics. You may think you're just being friendly with a coworker, but she may misinterpret your behavior. One thing may lead to another, and suddenly you're accused of harassment. At the other extreme, a more senior colleague may make sexual overtures toward you, and when you don't respond, you're passed over for promotion—or worse.

Sexual politics takes two major forms that you need to be aware of:

Sexual dynamics In the workplace, your behavior and dress should always be professional and you should not use sexual humor; you do not want to cross the thin line into appearing sexually provocative. You want to advance because of your skills and your contribution to your organization, not because you attract or arouse your coworkers—however subtly. Along the same lines, while it's perfectly normal to feel physical attraction to a colleague, or vice versa, you both need to be very careful of what comes next. Some companies have a "nonfraternization" policy, which discourages colleagues from dating each other, and flirting or other behavior that distracts you from work can damage your career.

Sexual harassment Sexual harassment is a crime. It is clearly defined by both state and federal laws as unwanted sexual advances, or visual, verbal, or physical conduct of a sexual nature that interferes with your ability to do your job. Some actions are clearly harassment, such as when your boss promises you a raise in exchange for some sexual favor. Other actions, which are less clear, are really in the eye of the beholder. So if you interpret some behavior to be sexual harassment, try to get some outside feedback before you move forward.

Survival strategies if you're the one who is "different"

■ Be prepared to pay the "tax" of being different. It can take longer to get where you want to go because it may take longer for people to learn to trust you. It may also take you longer to develop important relationships you need to get promoted and to get handed more responsibility.

■ Recognize you will often be held to a higher standard. And while you are working doubly hard, you may also have to take on tasks that the majority group can ignore: managing perceptions and misinterpretations, reading subtle signals, and surviving slights.

■ Take jobs that are central to the organization's work. These are the jobs that are the most valued and get rewarded. If it's primarily a sales company, get into sales. If it's manufacturing, get into operations. Avoid administrative positions where it can be harder to establish a track record based on your impact on the bottom line.

■ Know where you want to go and accept only the jobs that will move you in that direction. Resist being pigeonholed into jobs that are "good for diversity candidates," like HR or community outreach. Market yourself instead based on your unique skills, and be willing to take a lateral or backward step to get where you want to go.

■ Find a mentor and a **sponsor**. A mentor acts as a career adviser, providing inside info, reality checks, and emotional support. A sponsor is a colleague who uses his influence and power to help you advance your career. They act as your PR agents, recommending you for high-visibility task forces or presenting an explanation when your actions are questioned.

■ Don't take a slight personally, even when it is. Realize that society plays a major role in shaping stereotypes about diverse groups, and that these are what are at play here—not your unique personality.

Sexual Politics: Key Definitions

Sexual dynamics: The normal physical attraction that can occur between two people

Sexual harassment: Sexual behavior that makes one person feel uncomfortable, pressured, or victimized

Gendered expectations: When individuals act according to society's expectations about male or female behavior (see page 146)

dealing with discrimination

When you think
your employer is not
playing fair

When you don't get that promotion, it's easy to blame it on **discrimination**, particularly if you are a member of a group that is protected from discrimination under state and federal laws. These laws prohibit employment decisions from being affected by the candidate's mental or physical disability, national origin, ancestry, sex, age, pregnancy, race, or religious beliefs.

But before you claim discrimination and file a suit, take a hard, thoughtful look at the entire situation.

Ask yourself some tough questions What skills or knowledge did the new position require that you might not have had? Is there anything else you could have done better to sell yourself?

Ask your employer for insight Don't be afraid to come right out and ask why you didn't get the promotion. While many employers won't give you anything more than the standard "We promoted the best person," some will give you valuable feedback on ways you can improve your chances next time around.

Ask third parties outside of your workplace Describe what happened to someone inside and someone outside of your social identity group. Do they see it differently? How so?

If, after careful reflection, you decide that discrimination is at play here, you may decide to go forward. You'll need to do two things:

■ **Determine that you have a case** Legal action may be warranted if you can show proof that you were treated differently because of your social identity. (If your employer is simply rude or a jerk, you don't have a case.) Having documentation, such as an e-mail or letter, strengthens your case.

■ **File a claim** If you want to proceed, you'll need to file a complaint with the Equal Employment Opportunity Commission (EEOC), which has offices in all major cities. Find out more at **www.eeoc.gov**. If your finances allow, you may then want to seek out a labor attorney who specializes in these cases.

Job-Related Legislation

You and your job are protected against discrimination by the federal laws listed below. But check your specific state and city laws, because they supersede these federal laws. For example, in some states sexual orientation and obesity are protected by laws. Here's a rundown of federal legislation that may apply to you:

The Americans with Disabilities Act (1990)

Prohibits discrimination based on mental or physical disability, as long as those disabilities don't prevent you from doing the job. The act also requires the employer to provide reasonable accommodations, such as adaptive equipment, to enable you to perform critical job tasks.

The Immigration Reform and Control Act (1986)

Prohibits the employment of illegal aliens but also protects you against discrimination based on national origin or citizenship status.

The Age Discrimination in Employment Act (1978)

Prohibits discrimination against applicants aged 40 or older.

The Pregnancy Discrimination Act (1978)

Prohibits discrimination against pregnant women in the hiring process and during their employment. This also applies to women with pregnancy-related medical conditions.

The Civil Rights Act (1964)

Prohibits employment discrimination based on race, sex, national origin, ancestry, or religious beliefs.

physical challenges

Getting your needs met

If you are a physically challenged professional, you probably already know that the greatest obstacle you are likely to face in the workplace is getting colleagues to overcome their stereotypical thinking about people with disabilities. Even though you may have the skills, the knowledge, and the motivation to do the job, you may also have to convince your coworkers that your wheelchair, crutches, or teletype phone won't slow you down.

Building a strong performance track record and a network of crucial relationships are essential elements of career success, regardless of your physical abilities. But as a physically challenged employee, you also need to:

■ **Be open about your abilities and your disabilities** In this litigious and politically correct climate, bosses and colleagues may feel anxious about discussing your physical challenges. They may be more comfortable making assumptions about what you can and cannot do, which can stall your career. Preempt these assumptions by being forthcoming about the kind of support you need and don't need from your colleagues.

■ **Be prepared to request the accommodations you need** If it makes it any easier for you, realize that employers are usually pleasantly surprised when they find out how little it costs to cover most accommodations, such as a special office chair or keyboard: 80 percent of accommodations cost between $0 and $500.

FIRST PERSON SUCCESS STORY

Overcoming the fear of the unknown

When I was 45 I developed multiple sclerosis, and for about six months was in and out of work. Fortunately, my condition stabilized and I was able to go back to full-time work. The problem was that my colleagues and my boss weren't ready for me. They were very helpful and accommodating, but they also treated me as if I would fall apart if they overloaded me with work.

After two months of feeling like they were handling me with kid gloves, I asked my boss if I could have my doctor come in and speak to the members of my department. He agreed, and my department, without me present, met with her. She gave a brief overview of this progressive disease and then opened her talk up for questions. Apparently my colleagues asked some really good questions about my disorder and what they could expect from me, and what they could do to help me with my work. She explained that I would be fine and that if my symptoms became problematic, then I could take care of myself. She talked about the need to look at illness as a part of life, not something to hide or push aside. This apparently impressed a lot of my coworkers, some of whom were grappling with their own problems, such as a sick husband or a frail parent. And she gave them some literature to read if they wanted to learn about MS. After her talk, my colleagues felt more open about talking with me about my situation and I found I grew closer to them as they started to share stories of their own problems, health and otherwise. My boss was so impressed with the fallout from my doctor's presentation that he suggested I write it up and present it to the company's executive HR committee. I did, and since then they have asked for my input on HR issues. With this kind of support, I am thinking of switching over to HR and creating a new career path for myself.

—Jonathan S., Springfield, MO

now what do I do?

I heard through the grapevine that my boss described me as "rude" after I disagreed with him during a meeting—even though I did not raise my voice. What did I do wrong?

"Rude" is often code for "not following the rules." In your personal life, when you call someone rude, it is usually because they violated your rules for acceptable behavior (for example, by interrupting you or not thanking you for a present). The same is true in organizations. Most likely the boss called you rude because you didn't follow his rules for how to behave in a meeting. To repair that relationship, and to figure out the rules so that you can follow them the next time, ask your boss how he would like you to voice disagreement in the future. He may say that he would rather have you discuss your conflicting ideas with him in private, rather than in a large meeting. Working well with your boss is a vastly important ingredient in managing your career; see chapter 3 for more.

I am the only woman in sales at a tool and die company. The guys are always making jokes about women, and I feel really uncomfortable. What can I do?

If you don't feel comfortable telling them directly to stop making jokes, bump it up to HR or your boss. If you want to handle it yourself, realize that it will probably be easier for you to change them one by one, rather than taking on the entire group at once. "Divide and conquer" the group by telling each man individually how you feel about their jokes. Using humor can help them save face. (In one company, a woman who was offended by an office calendar of half-dressed women kept taking it down, but the male employees kept putting it back up. It wasn't until she hung a calendar with nearly naked guys on it that the men finally got the point and took both calendars down.) What's important is that you set your boundaries, tell your coworkers what they are doing (you can't expect them to guess), and then consistently insist on compliance.

In our department, everyone copies everyone on e-mails. I get at least 100 FYI e-mails a day! How can I tell my coworkers to take me off the FYI list without it seeming like I don't care about what they are doing?

You are smart to be careful in how you ask people to remove your name, and you need to be smart when criticizing this e-mail rule, too.

Rules like this FYI e-mail one may be counterproductive, but people are still expected to follow them. People who ignore the rules are often criticized for not being team players. A good strategy when going against a rule is to explicitly state what you are doing and why, specifically connecting your reason to the benefit to the organization. For example, you could bring this FYI practice up at a department meeting and say, "While I appreciate being kept in the loop, I have become overwhelmed with the number of FYI e-mails I receive. Reading them takes time and I get backed up on projects. I'd like for us as a department to think about an alternative way of keeping everyone informed."

Helpful Resources

WEB SITES

Women and Diversity WOW! Facts
www.ewowfacts.com/index.html

Black Enterprise Magazine's List of Best Companies for Minorities
www.blackenterprise.com

IMDiversity
www.imdiversity.com
At this site, "where careers, opportunity, and diversity connect," job seekers can post résumés, search for diversity-friendly companies, and connect with diverse professionals like them in subsections organized by ethnic background.

BOOKS

Talking from 9 to 5
by Deborah Tannen

You Just Don't Understand
by Deborah Tannen

Disappearing Acts
by Joyce Fletcher

Breaking Through: The Making of Minority Executives in Corporate America
by David Thomas and John Gabarro

Our Separate Ways: Black and White Women and the Struggle for Professional Identity
by Ella L.J. Edmondson Bell and Stella M. Nkomo

Leading in Black and White: Working Across the Racial Divide in Corporate America
by Ancella Livers and Keith Caver

Getting to the Top
by Carol Gallagher

Do's and Taboos around the World
by R.E. Axtell

Working with your boss

Getting to know your boss 56
The keys to this vital relationship

Managing the boss 58
Some crucial tips

Get in the boss's head 60
The only way to please is to know
what your boss wants

Earn a gold star 62
Become the employee your boss
can't live without

Common types of problem bosses 64
You can survive—and even thrive

When you have a difficult boss 66
What to do when your boss sits between
you and your next great job

Be your own PR agent 68
Why publicizing your successes
is so important

Use your reviews 70
Beyond the evaluation: selling yourself

Now what do I do? 72
Answers to common questions

getting to know your boss

Think back to those early days with your new boss, when you were most eager to learn what made her happy. But now that you know your boss better, you still need to focus on making her happy. To that end, try to see your boss as a human being, with both strengths and weaknesses. Use the interview skills that helped you read between the lines to help identify your boss's strengths and weaknesses. Here are some key characteristics to note:

Skills What skills or knowledge areas does your boss lack? What does your boss hate to do? These represent great opportunities for you to focus on and challenges for you to take on.

Motivation What is your boss trying to accomplish in the organization? What gets her excited? What are the challenges facing her department, and how can you help meet them?

Blind spots Where are the holes in your boss's networks? Where does communication break down?

Communication style How does your boss prefer to receive information: just in time or with a long lead time; regularly or on a need-to-know basis? How much information does your boss want: the big picture or complete details? In what format, written or verbal?

Decision-making style What decisions can you make unilaterally, and what decisions does your boss want to be involved in? Does your boss make decisions based on intuition or data? What does your boss need from you to make a decision (time, data, benchmarks, precedences)?

Work style Does your boss prefer to work alone or with people? Is your boss a morning or night person? Is there an open-door policy? Does your boss thrive in chaos or prefer structure and order?

Ask the Experts

My boss's supervisor called me into her office to ask whether I was interested in becoming her new assistant. This would be a great step for me, but what should I tell my current boss?

This is a politically difficult situation, especially if your own boss knows nothing about this offer. No matter what you decide to do, either your boss or your boss's boss is going to be unhappy. So what can you do? Tell your boss's boss that you want the job and negotiate a raise and your title. Then it is your new boss's responsibility to tell your old boss about your promotion. You can also offer to help train your replacement to try to ease the tension.

I just started a new job, and since I'm still learning the ropes, I'm hesitant to ask my boss if I can take some time off to attend the annual meeting of a national professional association. What's the best approach?

Ideally, you would have negotiated your attendance at this conference before you accepted your job. However, you can still make a solid argument for attending the meeting. Ask your boss for 20 to 30 minutes of her time, then give her some background on the conference and show her any related materials. Explain the job-related benefits of your attendance, which may include knowledge you can use on the job and your inclusion in a network of industry experts who may become important clients or allies.

If your boss does not think attending the conference would be worthwhile, for whatever reason, don't lose hope. Focus on future networking and development activities, such as company-sponsored training programs, and work on getting your boss's approval for these, being clear about the knowledge or skills you will gain via such opportunities.

managing the boss

Realize your boss is human, too

It's easy to think your boss has all the power in your relationship. But if you give her sole responsibility for establishing and maintaining a good working relationship, you are critically jeopardizing your career. Putting all the responsibility on her makes you totally dependent upon her to meet your needs for job resources, support, civility, respect . . . and job assignments and promotions.

Consider reframing how you view your relationship with your boss to take a more active role.

Your boss does not have all the power Consider this a partnership in which each side is dependent upon the other. But just how is the boss dependent upon you? Think about what her job would be like without you. Who would do your work? Sure, she could hire someone else, but that involves recruiting, interviewing, and training a new person. Most bosses don't have the time.

Your boss isn't perfect You can't assume (and demand) that she manages flawlessly. Usually she has been promoted because of her job skills, not her management experience. Requiring that she be perfect only sets you up for disappointment and frustration, and it denies you the opportunity to help her be successful, thereby building your value.

Your boss is not your adversary Most bosses aren't looking to squeeze as much out of you as they can. But most bosses *are* facing tremendous pressure to produce, so you're either "with her or against her." Consider positioning yourself as an **ally** in your boss's fight against too many demands and too little resources.

Take note: Managing your boss isn't about being manipulative or "brownnosing" for personal gain. It's about creating and maintaining a relationship that produces positive outcomes for your career, your boss's, and the organization.

Guiding principles for managing your boss

Clarify your boss's expectations. Learn to understand what your boss wants. Work with him to set performance goals every quarter and agree on ways to evaluate your progress. Then deliver on time, on budget, and to your boss's specifications.

Make your boss look good Deliver what he needs when he needs it. Identify and solve problems before they happen. Don't argue with or correct him in public. Accept that he will occasionally take credit for some of your work (the highest compliment!).

Earn his loyalty Adhere to your boss's priorities to show you respect his authority. Don't make the same mistake more than once. Prevent stalemates and arguments by offering several options for a decision.

Get constant feedback Ask your boss frequently (monthly, after a project), "How am I doing?" Don't accept a vague, "Fine." Ask for specifics: "Are you happy with the format I'm using to publicize monthly sales figures?"

Keep your boss in the loop Be sure your boss is kept apprised of your progress, and don't try to hide problems.

Don't waste your boss's time Try to solve small problems on your own, and plan out meeting agendas with your boss beforehand.

get in the boss's head

The more you know,
the more power
you have

The more you know about your boss, the easier it will be to create a relationship that allows both of you to succeed. To get him to sing your praises, you need to learn the following things about him, then respond to them:

Personal and organizational goals What is your boss trying to accomplish in his job? What excites him? What are the greatest challenges and opportunities facing him and his department?

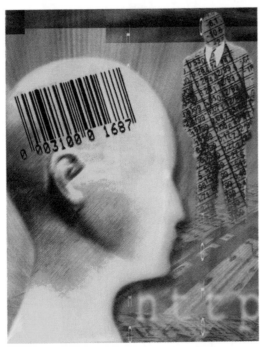

Pressures from his boss and peers What are the goals and priorities of your boss's boss and peers? What does his boss get angry about?

Performance measures What outcomes is he held accountable for? What standards, precedents, or measures are used to evaluate his success?

Strengths What skill or knowledge areas does your boss excel in?

Weaknesses What skill or knowledge areas does your boss lack? What does he hate to do? (These represent great opportunities for you to develop.)

Ask the Experts

How do I find out what matters to my boss?

Asking is the most straightforward and effective way. Request a meeting with your boss, and position the goal of the meeting as, "I'd like to learn about how you'd like me to work with you so that I can best meet your expectations. Can I ask you a few questions?" Then proceed through the list on the previous page. This is particularly important to do with a new boss: Don't assume your new boss will follow any of the same "rules" your old boss followed.

There is no way my boss will tell me what his priorities are or what he's worried about. He'll say, "I'll let you know as you need to know." Now what?

First, realize that he's telling you a lot about his needs and work style every day without saying a word. You just have to watch his behavior and put 2 and 2 together. The next time he gets upset about a project that's late, what have you learned? That speed and punctuality are very important to him. When he micromanages you on projects involving clients, but not internal ones, what does that tell you? That he values high-priority, high-profile projects that can help the company build a good reputation with customers over low-visibility ones, like ongoing administrative projects. When he keeps putting off a particular decision, what have you learned? This may be an area of low value to him, or an area that he doesn't like or isn't comfortable with. His questions will also give you valuable information. If he asks what could go wrong, for example, with a proposal you've made about restructuring how client projects are monitored as they move through the department, you can gain points in the future by always including contingency plans for any possible problems that could arise.

earn a gold star

Develop attributes bosses love

How do you stand out from the many people competing for your boss's attention? How do you earn "most valued employee" status, so that you are in a position for plum assignments and promotions? While all bosses want good results delivered on time and under budget, smart employees will follow these extra steps and earn the respect and appreciation of their bosses:

Be reliable Deliver results and follow through on commitments. Produce work that meets deadlines, specifications, and most important, your boss's expectations.

Be transparent Avoid surprises: Give your boss a "heads-up" when a project is running into trouble. Keep her informed of everything (good and bad) that is going on. Never let your boss get blindsided by information that should have come from you. Never mask your motives to your boss; always explain "why" so she understands that you're missing a meeting or a deadline because of work commitments, not personal ones.

Be proactive Uttering the words, "It's not my job," can be the kiss of death for your career. Actively seek out assignments beyond your job description by asking the boss, "What else can I do?" Come to him with ideas for new projects, persevere through roadblocks, and do whatever it takes to get the job done.

Be responsive Know what your boss's priorities and goals are, and work on the tasks that help him reach those goals. Always agree to his requests to show you're on "his side," but follow up with what you need to be able to deliver (for example, a longer time line, a deliverable of smaller scope).

Be optimistic Career-boosting new projects won't come your way if you always see the downsides of them. Your boss wants a problem solver, not a whiner. That doesn't mean that you shouldn't point out things that could go wrong, but always position your concern as a problem to be overcome. For example, "For us to be successful, let's think about how we can overcome XYZ roadblock."

Be responsible Take responsibility for your actions. Accept criticism, feedback, direction, and the blame for errors when due.

Be flexible Guard against becoming so attached to your work that you become resistant to change. Accept new procedures and initiatives willingly. Be an agent of change, not a resister. There's a fine line between preserving what works and being unreceptive to new ideas.

Be a team player No boss likes stepping in to referee a squabble between his direct reports. Resolve your own conflicts, come to consensus decisions, and give colleagues constructive feedback. Praise them to the boss when appropriate.

Be honest Your boss wants to be told the truth, but in a respectful way that follows his rules. Don't be afraid to state your opinions, but support them with data. Don't say "yes" if you mean "no," and don't overpromise on what you can deliver. If your boss asks you to do the impossible, let him know he's asking too much, but also provide an alternative. "I don't think I can do this in two weeks, but I can definitely do it in three."

Be low-maintenance Your boss has many people demanding her time and attention, so score big points by using her time sparingly. Bring solutions, not problems, and bring her options for a decision. Keep her informed of your work in an unobtrusive way (for example, through brief e-mail reports).

Be supportive Take the opportunity to thank your boss for his help on something or to give him positive feedback. Obviously, only sincere compliments will work here; anything less will seem like "brownnosing" or obsequious flattery.

common types of problem bosses

You can survive even the worst bosses

Most people encounter at least one aggravating boss during their careers. This is the boss who has one, possibly two very obvious shortcomings. You need to learn to recognize these shortcomings and how to navigate around them. Here's a primer:

The Avoider This boss puts off things she doesn't like, and often lets good ideas die from neglect. Overcome her inertia by offering to take the lead on projects. Once you do the "groundwork" that will create forward momentum, you will usually get her buy-in.

The Deadline Junkie Here, the boss starts working only if a deadline is looming. If that is the case, give him deadlines with some padding built in.

The Timid Mouse If your boss is risk-averse, then present decisions that need to be made with careful forethought; e.g., identify everything that could go wrong and create contingency plans. If the risk seems too big, identify how a "yes" decision might be tested out on a small scale first.

The Screamer If your boss favors intimidation tactics such as yelling, counter this by speaking very softly. If she likes to stand and confront you while you are seated, level the playing field by standing up.

The Micromanager This boss always needs to feel she's in control, so give her that by inundating her with information; e.g., by constantly sending updates and asking for feedback on every decision.

The "Sink or Swim" Boss You may feel that this boss doesn't "go to bat" for you. He may see it as a conflict he wants to avoid. Offer to fight the battle instead. Or he may be concerned about maintaining relationships. If so, build support for your ideas and get buy-in from others.

The Liar If you have a boss who lies or cheats, it's time to move on. You do not want to be associated with this kind of boss, because her lies will, at some point, involve you.

Ask the Experts

I like my work, but I have a do-nothing boss who blames me for his mistakes. What can I do to improve this situation?

First of all, realize that a "bad" boss is a person who doesn't know how to be a manager. Help him by managing the situation. Here are some how-to-manage-people strategies:

Reward the positive, ignore the negative It's important that your boss doesn't see how angry or frustrated he's made you. Instead, catch him doing something helpful and thank him, linking his positive behavior to how it helped you meet his needs.

Get what you need from others Seek out colleagues or talk with HR about getting the training or coaching you need.

Insulate yourself Minimize delays caused by your boss by becoming as autonomous as possible. Instead of asking for input into a decision, write in an e-mail, "I'm going to go with this vendor unless I hear otherwise."

Seek outside exposure Develop work and social relationships outside your department so people can distinguish between you and your current boss.

Know your limits Spend some time thinking about what you are willing to bear and what you will do if your boss ever crosses that line. Have an exit plan in place. You want to avoid staying with a boss who works against you for too long, or your next employer may wonder why you didn't advance.

when you have a difficult boss

Ways to get ahead if
your boss is blocking
your path

The biggest threat to your career is often the "toxic boss." This is a boss who is riddled with shortcomings. He not only takes credit for your work, but he also threatens you when you do anything that gets you noticed by upper management. In short, your success is poison to him—because in his mind, it only affirms his inadequacies. Thus, he constantly sets you up to fail. What can you do?

Ask yourself, "How have I contributed to the situation?" If your boss doesn't forward your ideas, could it be because you aren't persistent and creative in persuading him? Are you missing information about the organization's goals or about the priorities of your boss's boss that make your ideas unattractive? Are you treating him smugly or with scorn? Are you being a threat? Bullying and negative behavior go both ways. Answering these questions might yield a strategy for changing the situation.

Identify indirect strategies Ask yourself what you can do to work around the roadblock. For example, if your boss steals your ideas, put your name on everything, or spread your ideas beyond just your boss by telling colleagues or your mentor.

Jump over him as a last resort First, be aware of the perils of going to your boss's boss. Only do this when it's a battle you are willing to lose your job for. If your boss refuses to forward a brilliant idea, first ask him, "Is there anything else I can do to convince you to act before I take this up to your boss?" Even if you do win a "yes" from your boss's boss, you'll probably lose the relationship with your own boss. And some other senior managers may see you as disrespectful and unmanageable, too.

Learn and leave The safest recourse of all may be to learn from him how not to behave as a boss and move on. This may be the impetus you need to take an aggressive career step, and find a job that makes you happier.

Ask the Experts

My boss is like a "black hole": Ideas go in but they never come out. I can't believe senior management doesn't see this and fire her! What can I do?

Most likely management does see this, but is unwilling or unable to do anything about it. Your boss may be the CEO's daughter-in-law. Complaining up rarely results in a boss getting fired or moved, so in most cases, your only solution is to get out. Talk to HR about other opportunities and to your mentor or coach to get an outsider's perspective on the politics of the situation. Only in instances where the boss is involved in illegal activities (and then only with proper documentation and legal counsel) should you register your complaint with HR or senior management.

Last year I signed up for an advanced computer training course—twice. Both times, my boss made me cancel at the last minute, because of work deadlines. I still want to take the course, but I'm afraid of this happening again. What can I do?

To get to the root of this last-minute cancellation problem, analyze what is going on in your office. Are you the only one who has to cancel training plans, or does this happen to others, too? This will give you some sense of the scope of the problem. Then discuss with your boss how to handle the situation in the future, being careful not to play the "blame game." Plan who will take your responsibilities while you are out of the office and what will happen in case of an emergency.

If your boss does not respond well to this conversation, saying, for example, that he can't plan that far in advance, consider asking HR how bosses in other departments support employee training, and review with them the company training policy. If this policy is not being upheld, this may help you get your boss to commit the time and staff to cover you next time.

be your own PR agent

Promoting yourself is an essential job strategy

In the not-too-distant past, if you did good work and kept your nose to the grindstone, you eventually got promoted. Those days are gone. Competitive market forces are moving too quickly to wait for good work to be rewarded with an eventual promotion. Promotions are rarely given these days; in this competitive environment, you have to ask for them.

To get ahead, you need to aggressively market yourself and publicize your accomplishments—every day. Why? Because every day your boss is held accountable for how she is using the company's resources. Every day she is looking at her employees and deciding who is contributing to the bottom line and who isn't, and whose job could be outsourced or eliminated. This means that every day you need to remind your boss that her decision to hire you was a brilliant one—especially if you plan on asking for a raise or a promotion someday. Here are two strategies for "tooting your own horn" effectively:

Identify how you are adding value How is each of your tasks helping the company reach its goals? Consider how your tasks bring about:

■ **Financial benefits** How have you saved money, reduced costs, or generated profits?

■ **Productivity benefits** How have you streamlined tasks, decreased errors, or produced more with less?

■ **Image benefits** How have you made customers or clients happy, improved relations with vendors or unions, or resolved conflict between departments?

Let people know your value Make sure everyone sees all the great work you do. Most are too busy with their own "to do" lists to see all the things you've crossed off yours. You've got to tell them. See pages 69–70 for tips on how to do that.

Strategies for marketing yourself

Put your name on every document you produce Put a footer on every page that identifies you as the author or a contributor.

Use "weekly" or "status" reports as a marketing tool State your accomplishments, identify and quantify the results you produced, and include how the organization benefited from your activity.

Get your name on team output Never be shy about asking to be listed in the report or in the presentation.

Make the presentation If you've been working with a team, volunteer to make the final presentation; whoever does this "owns" the accomplishment.

Ask for feedback When you've completed a project or task, ask your boss about areas for improvement and areas in which you did well. As your boss points out the things you did well, he will at the same time be reminding himself of your value.

Accept a compliment When you are praised for you work, instead of saying, "Oh, it was nothing . . . " say, "Thank you. I'm pleased you recognized the work I put into the project."

Take ownership of your ideas If you make a suggestion in a meeting that is ignored, then someone else says it and gets credit for it, say, "Oh, Sam, I'm glad you thought my idea was worthwhile."

use your reviews

For most employees, hearing "It's time for your annual job review" fills them with anxiety about their performance. If you can, try to turn your thinking around and treat your performance appraisal as an opportunity to remind your boss about what a great employee you are. Here's how:

Review your accomplishments throughout the year If you have been faithfully keeping a file of those documents that show off your talents, you are in good shape. See page 12 for how to start a file of status reports you've written, e-mails outlining client outcomes, and anything else that discusses your work. Include thank-you's you've received from people. And be sure to keep a list that you add to every time you complete a project.

Create "success stories" In preparation for your job review, spend some time looking over what you've done and formulate brief **success stories**—accounts that include the situation, the problem or challenge you faced, the action you took, the results you produced, and the benefits to the organization. For more on success stories, see page 141.

Complete review forms thoroughly In many organizations, both the employee and the boss complete sections of the performance appraisal form. If that's true in your organization, take the time to fill it out completely. Beware of being overly critical of yourself. In many cases, employees rate themselves much lower than their bosses do.

Speak to your strengths A mistake that many employees (often women) make is to focus on what they did poorly. During the review meeting, if your boss compliments you on what a great job you did on a project, try not to undercut this by pointing out ways in which you failed, such as by stating, "Yes, I did do a good job on that, but I didn't reach my revenue target on it."

Thank your boss When bosses contribute positively to your accomplishments, use the review meeting to give them positive feedback and thank them for their support.

Ask the Experts

In several of my projects this past year I missed some major deadlines. I know the boss will bring this up. What should I do?

It's normal and expected that you'll have strengths and weaknesses. But handle the weaknesses smartly, and you'll still be seen as a valued employee. Frame a weakness as a need for professional development. Be proactive: Don't wait for your boss to bring it up. Instead, suggest to your boss that you'd like to make time management one of your developmental goals, and request training to improve the skill.

My boss tells me I'm terrific. I get all top ratings. Does that mean I don't have to market myself to her anymore?

Not necessarily. Rather, your boss may not value or understand the job review process or is uncomfortable with giving negative feedback. If she says, "You did a great job on this project," ask, "What specifically did I do well so I make sure I do it again in the next project?" As she answers that question, she'll be reminded of how terrific you are.

FIRST PERSON SUCCESS STORY

Going after feedback

I had worked for my same boss for four years and never got a performance appraisal or any kind of feedback. Not knowing how I was doing was driving me nuts, so I finally decided to ask him for feedback on how I present my data. I knew he would say, "It's just fine," so first I explained why I was asking for the feedback. I said, "I'd like for you to tell me how I could make this project report clearer. That way it will be easier for the board to see the results of our survey." But when even that elicited a vague reply, I had to get specific and ask, page by page, "What about this?" and "Do you think it would be better this way?" Finally I dragged some good information out of him and was actually able to improve my document.

—Hugh M., Baton Rouge, LA

now what do I do?

Answers to common questions

A year ago my boss chose not to proceed with a new software system. It turned out to be a bad decision. How do I get my boss to change his mind when he views any suggestion as a challenge to his authority?

Let go of the past and focus on the future. It's better not to revisit the old decision, pointing out factors that were ignored or assumptions that proved erroneous. If you appear to be forcing him to face up to a bad decision, he'll only get defensive and become more resistant to changing his mind. Instead, position the old decision as "the best at the time." No one responds well to an "I told you so" attitude. Suggest that a new decision is called for because things have changed: What new information is there? What new needs have developed? "Blaming" the need for a new decision on factors external to his control allows him to change his mind without losing face.

I constantly have to cover for my boss. He'll disappear from the office for several hours and miss meetings. One time I even caught him asleep in his office. Should I keep covering up his mistakes?

If your boss were engaging in illegal practices, the answer would be simple: Go to the authorities. But like many employees, you face a muddier situation: You have a boss who is using work time for personal errands. The answer is less clear. You may choose to cover for your boss to prevent small embarrassments, such as by telling a caller, "He's in a meeting," when he's really sleeping. But over time this can become uncomfortable. The best solution is to talk to him about it. Describe the situation and its impact on you. For example, say, "I'm uncomfortable telling people that you are in a meeting when you are out of the office, golfing." Offer an alternative (you could transfer the calls to his cell phone) but be firm that you won't continue the cover-up. If he makes your life miserable as a result, talk to Human Resources or look for another job. This isn't a boss you want to work for.

My boss has just asked me to step down as team leader from a very visible project. I've never been demoted before. Should I start looking for a new job?

It's not surprising that you're thinking of leaving; after all, isn't a demotion an indication that you have no future in the company? Not necessarily. A demotion usually indicates that your work isn't up to expectations and that your boss wants you to improve. Regain the boss's confidence by first accepting that your work has to improve. Get over denying that it wasn't your fault or being angry that all your hard work wasn't recognized. Ask yourself some hard questions: Has your performance dropped off? Why? Does it tell you that you are bored with the job and should move on? Next, have a serious talk with your boss. Tell her you want to improve and together map out how that will happen. Clarify what your performance has to look like in order to regain the pay or the title that was taken away and set a target date. Many people say that a demotion, in hindsight, is a great wake-up call. Just try not to need waking up more than once during your career.

Helpful Resources

WEB SITES

"Managing Your Boss"
www.healthyplace.com/Communities/Anxiety/work _5.asp
"Managing Your Boss" by Marilyn Puder-York, Ph.D., gives tips for dealing with the prototypical difficult boss. Also links to articles on stress in the workplace.

SeekingSuccess.com
www.seekingsuccess.com
The "Career Articles" section of this site has great advice on getting ahead in your career and getting along with your boss.

BOOKS

Never Wrestle with a Pig
by Mark McCormack

How to Shine at Work
by Linda Dominguez

Beyond Performance
by Roland Nolen

Managing your colleagues

Office politics 76
Be helped, not hurt, by them

Types of politics 78
Know what to look out for

Problem colleagues 80
Know who you're dealing with

Feedback 82
Listen to learn what you need to know

Pulling your weight 84
Freeloading is not an option

Handling differences 86
You need everyone's support

The art of negotiating 88
Learn how to get what you want

Disagree with diplomacy 90
Get your point across without losing points

Conflict management 92
The art of repairing fences

Now what do I do? 94
Answers to common questions

office politics

Believe it or not, **office politics** is actually a strategy people use to compete for scarce resources, consciously or not. What are some of those scarce resources? Money, people, time, and status: money to fund projects; people to help with those projects; time with the boss; and, as you move up the career ladder, the scarcest resource of all, status, which is gained by participating in high-visibility projects with upper management.

Without enough of these resources, office politics is inevitable. When people are forced to compete, the result can be shifting coalitions, private agreements, and bargaining. Even if you find such competition distasteful, the solution is not to keep your head down, do your work, and try to stay invisible. This strategy may take you out of the competition for resources, as well as for promotions. It's tough to get ahead when you sit on the sidelines. Your goal is to become **politically savvy** in the office. That means recognizing the power dynamics in relationships with your colleagues—and learning how to capture some of those scarce resources.

Influence the Influencers

These tips will help you avoid the potential conflicts of office politics:

Align yourself with important people Keep company heavyweights informed of your activities, serve on their committees, and e-mail them news articles of interest. Coworkers will think twice about going after you, since it will mean going up against your allies.

Walk your own talk If you want people to listen to you, don't interrupt. If you want people to be honest with you, don't say "yes" when you mean "no." Follow through on commitments, give credit where credit is due, and don't pass the blame.

Cover yourself Keep records of all your correspondence on projects, especially when you feel a coworker is being unsupportive of the project. One tactic is to CC other people on e-mails to problem coworkers.

Look for red flags If your name was not included on several key meeting lists, this is a red flag. Start by asking, "Why is my name not on this meeting list?" Ask around to uncover motives and force coworkers to make the real message explicit. And if their intent was malicious, it stops the game by letting them know you're aware of what's going on.

Keep an open mind Before jumping to conclusions, get the full story. And don't take things personally. Plenty of things are said and done out of ignorance or insensitivity, rather than malicious intent. Finally, don't act in anger. Calm down first and decide on the best course of action.

types of politics

Recognize the enemy

Office politics can take several forms, and all of them can be damaging to your career if you act on impulse rather than thinking things through. You need to think long term and respond in a constructive way that preserves your reputation and working relationships over the long run, not just in this one instance. Here are tips for doing just that when it comes to common workplace skirmishes:

Backstabbing A colleague reveals to you that Jack from another department is telling his team untruths about you. This calls for a quiet, private confrontation. Be direct and say, "Jack, I hear that you've been saying I'm the reason our project was late. Why are you saying that?" You goal is first to see if you are getting correct information (your colleague could be exaggerating things). If it is true, then your goal is not to "prove him wrong," but to bring his motivation out into the open. Chances are, simply asking "why" will stop him in his tracks. If it doesn't, let it go. Avoid escalating things by taking it public or to the boss. This will only serve to set Jack up to retaliate. However, if it happens again, then cover yourself and talk to your boss.

False rumors Jim tells you he heard Carmen dropped the ball with a client. You know this is wrong and immediately correct Jim, but should you also tell Carmen about the rumor? Wait. First, mention to Jim that you will tell Carmen about this false rumor if he doesn't. If he doesn't, then tell her what you've heard—and from whom, and move on. Now it's Carmen's battle, not yours.

Gossip overload Erica's constant stream of gossip redefines the "grapevine" as the "sewer line." You need to disconnect from a coworker who is so full of negativity. But do it carefully: You don't want to be added to her list of topics. The next time Erica starts dishing, interrupt and excuse yourself—"Erica, I value our friendship, but this is making me uncomfortable"—or find a diplomatic way to cut the conversation short. You then might want to physically remove yourself from her. This allows her to save "face" while setting necessary boundaries around the relationship.

Passed over You find out that Andrea was handed the plum assignment you wanted. You could rant and rave to your friends about how you're more qualified, but a smarter approach is to meet with the decision-maker to ask for feedback: "Would you be willing to share with me why I was not selected for this project? This will help me identify the skills I need to develop for future opportunities." This positions you as a go-getter, not a whiner. Keep the feedback to yourself and work on these skills. Other opportunities will arise eventually.

Unethical behavior You witness Frank manipulating his time sheet. Doing nothing connotes tacit approval and makes you an accomplice, but informing on Frank will have serious consequences, so take cautious steps. First, make sure your facts are completely straight. Second, tell Frank what you've witnessed and ask him for an explanation. He may be acting on information unknown to you. For example, his boss may have told him to add on some extra weekend hours. If he admits what he did is wrong, ask him how he will rectify it. Keep the ball in his court; Frank should tell his boss, not you. If Frank hedges, tell him you must notify his boss. If he still won't do it, then you must move forward.

Sexist or racist jokes During lunch, a colleague tells a sexist or racist joke. You laugh along, figuring that because there are no women or people of color in the group, no one can be offended. Right? Wrong. Laughing at these types of jokes signals that you are in agreement with the underlying prejudices. That is not the reputation you want to have. Initiate a one-on-one discussion with the joke-teller and explain that she really should be careful unless she wants to be known as racist or sexist. If the jokes continue, find others to have lunch with.

problem colleagues

Know how to navigate
around their demands

Take a good look around your workplace. No matter what industry you work in, your workplace is probably made up of a number of familiar character types. First, there are all the "gold star" employees: the ones who work hard, get along with everyone, and are generally pleasant to be around. If you're lucky, your workplace consists almost entirely of these types.

But like most companies, yours probably has its share of problem employees. There's the one who never finishes what she starts. The one who complains endlessly. And so on . . .

Navigating office politics successfully requires you to have the inside scoop on these problem colleagues. You need to know what motivates them, what resources are most valuable to them, and how they prefer to work. Once you know that, you need to develop a set of response mechanisms so you can create the smoothest working relationship possible with them.

This is easier than you might think, because most problem employees come in just a few types. The ones in your workplace may differ superficially in some ways from the ones described on page 81, but the fact remains that, just as office politics everywhere assumes the same basic forms (backstabbing, gossiping, etc.), so too do difficult coworkers, and so too should your methods for dealing with them.

Common types of problem colleagues

The Gossiper The best way to deal with gossipers is to avoid them if you can, but if you can't, don't hesitate to tell them that you're not interested in their info. Do not pass their news on, and do not discuss anything of importance with them. Once they realize you're not interested, they will move on to someone who is.

The Know-It-All Colleagues who think they are always right about everything are in desperate need of ego reinforcement. Preempt their need to disruptively display their expertise by asking them to present at a meeting or asking for their opinion up front. If they are wrong, correct them in private.

The Perfectionist These people will haunt you with their red pens or calculators until you explode. If you must deal with them, set ground rules about what is realistic to expect and what isn't. Put boundaries on the amount of time you'll give them to review your work. And don't take it personally—they find fault with everybody, even themselves.

The Whiner Like black storm clouds, whiners cast a shadow over the workplace and kill morale. When working with them, don't try countering every complaint. Instead, ignore their negative comments. Walk away, don't join in the kvetching, and don't try to cheer them up. Make it known that people need to approach you with solutions, not problems.

The Victim In the minds of victims, management is always out to get them by overworking them or passing them up for promotions. Instead of taking some of the victim's workload just to get him to go away, "outvictim" the victim with your own tales of woe. This will usually bore him enough that he will seek sympathy elsewhere.

The Faultfinder These colleagues are never satisfied and will hold up projects with incessant critiques. To stop this behavior, explain that if they are going to find fault with something, it's fine for them to point it out, but only if they also provide a suggested fix, too.

The Change Hater Usually an employee who's been around forever, the change hater will do everything he can to prevent new ideas and practices from being implemented. If you're the one who has to make the changes, be nice but stick to your guns. Show him that management is on your side with official memos or e-mails. Figure out how this change will benefit him. Break the change into small steps, or get a "yes" by promising to revisit the decision down the road.

feedback

Being open to a
"report card" will keep
you in the game

Meeting the needs and expectations of your boss and colleagues is essential to being seen as valued and promotable. Positive and negative feedback are critical to advancing your career.

So how do you get the feedback you need from them? Ask for it. Don't wait for annual performance reviews. Regularly ask your boss and colleagues, "What can I do differently that will better support your work?" You should also ask for positive feedback (especially from the person who only sees the negative!). No, you're not looking for a pat on the back. You're asking them to tell you what you're doing right, so that you can continue that behavior.

If you get negative feedback, resist the urge to get defensive or argue with them about it. Breathe deeply and listen. When they are finished, thank them. That goes for positive feedback, too. Reward people for giving you feedback by actively listening, thanking them, and explaining how you will use their feedback to change your behavior.

Recognize that you are getting implicit feedback all the time. One coworker rolls his eyes whenever you make a suggestion. Another sighs heavily when you go on and on in a meeting. And this one never returns your e-mails. These are all signals that your behavior isn't working. Most people ignore those red flags because it's easier to believe there is no problem, or if there is a problem, that it's not their fault. These are the same people who are shocked when the promotion doesn't come—or the pink slip does.

Ask the Experts

Our team leader told me that several of my team members feel I'm not very committed to our project. I couldn't believe my ears. What do I do with feedback I totally disagree with?

Thank her for her feedback (which doesn't imply you agree with it) and ask if she'd like to hear your perspective on the situation. If she says "no," talk to your teammates to figure out if you were wrong. If she says "yes," discuss the issue with her, and ask her what you can do to change their perception.

FIRST PERSON SUCCESS STORY

Getting a colleague to sing my praises

For my first five years at a research institution, I had a great relationship with the president. Then a new president came in. I thought I'd be fine and I'd still have the same access. I walked into his office on his second day and he was on the phone and shooed me out. I knew things had changed. Pretty quickly I realized he didn't think much of my work. Because I had little direct interaction with the president, I had little opportunity to show him my work. But by doing good work with a senior colleague, slowly I got a chance to prove myself to him. Still, I needed more support to really gain his trust. I asked this colleague, who worked with the president frequently, to run an active "public relations campaign" for me. She would often point out to the president what great work I had done. Over time, the president came to respect my contributions, and it was all because of my "champion" singing my praises.

—Brian D., Dayton, OH

pulling your weight

Think like an accountant

One of the rules of the office is that everyone should do his work, or "pull his own weight." Ideally, everyone works hard and manages to do his work on time. Most coworkers will pitch in if you need help with your work from time to time—especially if you have legitimate reasons such as illness or an excessive workload. But if this becomes a chronic problem, then watch out. Those who continue to shirk their work—regardless of the reason—are bound to be labeled as freeloaders.

To sidestep this, treat your relationships as you would a bank account, where you deposit and withdraw favors. Whenever you have an interaction with a colleague, you are either paying into or debiting your account with that colleague. For example, when you meet a colleague's deadline or praise her in a meeting, your account with that person is credited. On the other hand, when you give negative feedback or fire off a terse e-mail, your account is debited.

For your credits to count, however, you need to give colleagues things that are important to them, so tune in to what makes each one tick. For example, you may love recognition, but when you publicly thanked a colleague who helped you with your project, he was embarrassed. Your effort to pay him back with praise just cost you instead. He might have preferred to have been paid back with private thanks or help on his project. Remember, your goal is to have your accounts between you and your colleagues in relative balance.

What to put in coworkers' accounts

A colleague has really helped you out at work. How do you pay him back? To figure out the best approach, simply ask him, "What can I do for you to show my thanks?" Here's a list of what coworkers really want:

Affiliation (being part of a group) Sometimes all that is needed is to include your helpful coworker in your group. Next time ask him to go to lunch with you and the gang.

Visibility (working on key projects that have high visibility with management) Another payback is to offer a chance to work on the next visible project that you are assigned.

Recognition (where her name is on the documents or her input is clearly acknowledged) This is a smart and easy payback. Always ask a coworker if she wants her name involved with the project she is helping on.

Resources Do you have resources (information, skills, connections to other people) that he could use in his other projects?

Personal support When you work together, is it all business—with no time spent connecting as people and sharing concerns about your professional and personal lives? Sometimes simply being friendly is all that is required.

handling differences

Colleagues can impede you as you strive to do good work and get promoted, or they can help you succeed. It's a good idea to look at your colleagues as whole people with whom you have likes and differences. Your goal is to understand both and use both to one another's mutual advantage. For instance, one of your coworkers has great skills and always delivers . . . but at the last minute. You need to learn to address how his work style is different from yours. Here are strategies to use to help you handle how coworkers approach their work differently:

Resist labeling If you label your coworker a "procrastinator," he becomes the enemy. Instead, recognize that this behavior probably makes total sense to him. He may feel he does his best work against a deadline.

Accept your differences You and your coworker have your own guidelines for behavior. If one of your rules is to start assignments early, it's tempting to consider your coworker's rushed approach a "wrong" or "bad" rule. Instead, think of it as "different."

Anticipate how he will view you Just as you think your coworker is a "procrastinator," he is probably labeling you "anal-retentive." To avoid a negative label, explain your own behavior so he won't mis-interpret your motives. For example: "If I wait until the deadline, I get too stressed to think clearly. I need to start earlier."

Work with your differences To improve teamwork, emphasize to your coworker how you can support team efforts in different ways. For example, you can keep a project running smoothly with your good time-management skills, and he's great in a crisis.

Find a reasonable solution You can learn to live with your coworker's lateness (and learn not to panic), or try to per-suade him to start projects earlier.

Try to compromise You won't bug him, and he will start work on a task at least three days before the deadline. Whatever you decide, make sure it's fair and agreeable to both of you.

It's about respect and time

Most differences about work are caused by different sets of internal rules regarding respect and time—two critical resources all coworkers need and want.

Establishing respect

Luke's view "I always stop by Joe's desk in the morning to get an update on our clients. But when I ask, 'How is everything this morning?' he'll just answer, 'Fine.' What's his problem?"

Joe's view "Luke always shows up at my desk, interrupts my work, and wants to ask for details on all our clients. Doesn't he have work to do?"

What's going on? The way to capture Joe's respect is through individual hard work. The way for Luke is connecting verbally about business matters. Luke's "How's it going?" isn't a bid to avoid work, but a necessary step to do work by getting the details on client relationships first.

What should they do? They need to share their respective rules for establishing respect and ideally find a middle ground. For example, they agree that a five-minute update each morning is okay, and after that they both need to attend to their own work.

The meaning of "urgent"

Sasha's view "Charlotte and I work together on client accounts. I respond quickly to Charlotte's e-mail requests, but she drags her feet on mine. Even if I flag it as 'urgent,' it still takes her days to get back to me."

Charlotte's view "Sasha is demanding and impatient. She always complains that I don't reply to her e-mails fast enough. I always do it as soon as I have a free minute, but it's not fast enough for her."

What's going on? Charlotte and Sasha have very different definitions of "urgent." Sasha's "urgent" means "right this second," while to Charlotte it means as soon as she has time.

What should they do? They need to clarify their differences and agree on some mutual rules. What will "urgent" mean for the two of them and what is an acceptable response time? Both will probably have to compromise.

the art of negotiating

You undoubtedly know how important **negotiating** is while you are securing a new job and angling for a higher salary and more benefits. But what some people fail to realize is that negotiating is an everyday activity that will assure their career success, especially when it comes to dealing with colleagues.

Think back to a sticky problem you had with a colleague. How did you handle it? Chances are you worked out some sort of solution that called for some negotiating skill. Why not apply the full art of negotiating when you have conflicts? Here is how you can turn conflicts into negotiated opportunities:

Prepare in advance Doing your "homework" is an essential element of successful negotiating. It is critical that you know what you want and what you are willing to forgo. You will also want to learn as much as you can about the other person—for example, their needs and pressures.

Identify in advance several options that might satisfy both of your needs Remember that negotiating is a process of reaching a happy medium. Put yourself in your coworker's shoes and try to identify exactly where she is coming from, and what you can do to at least meet her halfway.

Manage your emotions The management of your emotions before, during, and after a negotiation is vital. Ego, revenge, and one-upmanship should have no role in negotiations.

Negotiating 101

Speak up Men often think of negotiating as a game. Women, on the other hand, often fear alienating others if they speak up. Know that you can advocate for yourself and still stay on good terms with people in your organization. In fact, negotiating well often strengthens relationships.

Take your time Instead of saying "yes" or "thank you" when the first offer has been made, ask, "May I have time to think about that?" With that simple statement, you have signaled that you intend to bargain.

Be prepared to wait for a response to your request Taking time to respond is a standard negotiating tactic. When facing silence, you might be tempted to reduce your demands. Don't.

Once the negotiation process is over, assess how well you did. Did you get movement on one or two of your critical issues? Did the other side make statements such as, "Okay, I hear what you are saying, I can give more time to the project, but only for the next month"? If so, then it sounds as if you were successful. Congratulate yourself for beginning to develop one of life's critical skills.

disagree with diplomacy

Voicing differences with tact

During a meeting, you and a colleague disagreed on how to change an operating policy. Days later, you are horrified to hear stories going around about how you had "assaulted" her in the meeting. Word even got up to your boss, who demanded to know, "Why can't you two just get along?"

How did a **disagreement** (a difference in opinions, perspectives, or ideas) escalate into such a negative situation? You didn't yell in the meeting, name-call, or use profanity; you simply presented an alternative option.

Disagreements often create loaded situations because even though you know rationally that the work benefits from different perspectives, emotionally you may fear the consequences of disagreeing. Everyone wants to win and be right, because when others agree with you, you feel valued.

When others disagree with you, however, you may feel that your competence or reputation is being questioned. Disagreement is known to trigger the "fight or flight" response, because on some level you (or your colleague with whom you are disagreeing) feel threatened. When that happens your body goes into automatic reflex actions: short, shallow breathing, increased blood flow to the muscles, decreased blood flow to the brain and stomach.

When this fight or flight response is triggered some people go into attack mode, while others withdraw, saying "yes" when they actually mean, "I give up." Both responses can hurt work relationships, not to mention result in a decision that doesn't have full buy-in. How then do you disagree? The first thing to do is learn the rules for disagreeing in your organization. Watch how successful people in your organization disagree and mirror them. Do they agree in public or private? Do they speak loudly or softly? Do they offer a "better" idea or a "different" idea?

Strategies for keeping your cool
—and your position

Pause—before you respond Instead of automatically getting angry with someone or something, recognize your anger and ask yourself: "How do I wish to respond?" By making your responses deliberate and mature, you gain much more control over your emotions.

Disagree with the position, not the person Avoid personal attacks. Instead of saying, "I disagree with you," frame it as "I disagree with your idea." Avoid value-laden words like "wrong" and "bad," as well as "your" and "my," which create a divide. Use neutral words like "interesting" and phrases like "Let me offer a different idea . . . "

Reinforce the contributor's value Say, "I hear what you're saying . . . " or "I see that you've put great thought into this . . . " or "I appreciate your point of view . . . " This further separates the person from her position.

Position the two of you on the same side It's not you against them; it's the two of you against a common problem. Acknowledge your mutual goal of making the best decision possible by using "we" instead of "I."

Don't hit it head-on Instead of negating a position, build on it. "I like your idea. Let's go one step further and . . . " Find ways of integrating components from the other position into yours.

Know when to "fold 'em" At some point you have to ask yourself, "Is it better to win than to maintain this relationship . . . or to keep my job?" Choose your battles wisely.

Be a gracious winner or loser Once the decision has been made, accept it. If your idea didn't prevail, let it go, get on board, and put all your energy into implementing the decision. Continuing to disagree can be fatal to your career. If your idea did prevail, be humble and give others their due credit.

conflict management

To stay competitive, organizations are downsizing, merging, restructuring, and cost-cutting. That often means producing more with less in a shorter amount of time with fewer resources with a diverse group of colleagues. Under these pressures, it doesn't take much to ignite workplace conflicts. Nothing will set your career back like a blowup with a coworker. So be proactive and try to prevent flare-ups in the first place.

Avoid lighting your own fuse Understand how you respond to difficult situations, such as someone criticizing your work or presenting an alternative to your suggestion. Do you see it as an

affront? One way to avoid escalating the situation is to try to not see the world through a win-lose competitive frame. Your suggestion doesn't have to prevail completely for you to "win."

Slow down your "fight or flight" response When you feel threatened, do you tend to attack immediately, or withdraw and begin plotting revenge? Either one will only serve to escalate things, so take a breather and take control of your instincts.

Don't second-guess others' intentions They may be acting in their own best interests and with no thought about how it will impact you. Or they may just be acting spontaneously with no calculated intent. Sometimes a different opinion is just that—a different opinion.

Appreciate differences Conflict is often about wanting the other person to be more like you. "Why can't they just see it my way?" should alert you that you're viewing different ideas as barriers. Instead, try to recognize that differences actually present more options for you to choose from.

Picking up the pieces

Sometimes conflicts are inevitable. Here are some strategies to build bridges:

Ask your colleague if he would like to try to work things out It takes two to tango. If he says, "No," ask "Why not?" His response to conflict may be to withdraw, so help him see how the work and relationships will benefit by resolving it.

Decide when and where to talk about things If tempers are red-hot, suggest that everyone cool off first. When possible, have the conversation in private. No one will back down in front of other people.

Together set the rules of engagement If you were both yelling before, agree that you will avoid yelling or threats. Agree on some do's: Do ask for a time-out when feeling overwhelmed; do stick to the one issue under discussion (this avoids dumping an entire history of grievances into one conversation); do listen without interrupting.

Together define the problem This allows you to see all sides of the story. What isn't working? What still is working? (That question helps you see that this isn't the end of the world, and there are still some good aspects to work and the relationship.) Why did you take that action? (That question reveals the information and motivations your colleague was acting on.)

Minimize the time spent reconstructing history The purpose isn't to figure out who screwed up or who started the conflict. The more time you spend talking about the past, the more it will feel like you are trying to assign blame, which only makes people defensive and dig into their positions.

Focus on the future How would we like things to be? This moves you into problem-solving. Come up with as many options for moving forward as possible.

Together decide how this conflict will be avoided in the future Use this conflict as an opportunity to identify what needs to change (both in terms of how the work is organized and how people interact with each other) to avoid the same conflict in the future.

Note: Your conflict won't be resolved unless all affected parties want to resolve it. If one person wants to perpetuate it (either by pretending it doesn't exist or by refusing to try to work things out), then the conflict can't be resolved. Sometimes one person may perpetuate the conflict as a way of getting control or attention. If that's the case, document your efforts and, as a last resort, consider bumping the matter up to your boss.

now what do I do?

My coworker is always trying to unload her work on me. How do I say "no" to her and still look like a team player?

While you want to maintain your reputation of being the "go-to" person—the one who is always willing to pitch in and do whatever it takes to get the job done—you also need to guard against getting into work relationships that are not reciprocal. One way to do this is to say "no" by instead saying, "Yes, but . . ." As in: "Yes, I can help, but then I'll need your help finishing up my task." Doing this demonstrates your willingness to help, but attaches a cost to your help that she may not be willing to pay.

My colleague constantly changes her mind, which wreaks havoc on the work I do. How do I tell her she's making my life miserable?

Don't simply go up to her and state your case. You want her to buy into your concerns. Approach her and ask if she would like to get some feedback about her work style. If she says "no," she probably wouldn't have listened in the first place. If she says "yes," describe the behavior and the negative impact it has on you. For example, "When you change your mind after a decision has been made, I often have to go back and redo work. This is frustrating to me as it means I spend twice the time on a task." Where possible, include how her behavior doesn't help her either: "This means you have to wait longer for me to deliver the finished product." Suggest ways to change this behavior and ask for her ideas, too.

I was out ill for a few weeks, and then I took some vacation time. I sense several of my colleagues are angry at the extra work they had to take on because of my absence. What can I do?

Once the workload gets out of balance—no matter what the reason—some colleagues will attempt to even up the accounts. How? Your e-mails may go unanswered. Your requests for assistance or input may be ignored. In short, your ability to persuade and obtain support will be seriously compromised. The only way to remedy this is to do something for them to right the balance by offering them some form of "repayment." For example, thank them explicitly for their help. Then offer to help out with their work.

Since the birth of my second daughter I have been telecommuting. I am worried that being out of sight will keep me out of the loop. What can I do to show my colleagues that I am still on the team?

Be in touch often Regularly check in via e-mail.

Be available Set up specific times for a regular phone conference or conversation. That way you don't have to rely on catching (and missing) busy coworkers.

Be flexible If a meeting gets switched to one of your home days, try to come in that day and stay home another.

Be creative Attend important meetings via speakerphone or videoconference technology.

Be social Relationships are still best developed through face time, so use social events to make up for some of those water cooler conversations you've missed.

Helpful Resources

WEB SITES

Simmons College
www.simmons.edu/~fox/netiquette.html
Links you to many sites outlining etiquette on the Internet.

Vault
www.vault.com
Tips for working with colleagues.

Texas State
www.careeerservices.swt.edu/Student_Alumnus/ Job_Search_Manual
Avoid offending people with this page of links on business etiquette.

Careers by Design
www.careers-by-design.com/tki.asp
Learn your own responses to conflict and how you can manage them better by taking the world's leading conflict diagnostic test, the Thomas-Kilmann Conflict Mode Instrument (TKI). Cost is $30.

BOOKS

Influence Without Authority
by Allen Cohen and David Bradford

The Platinum Rule
by Tony Alessandra and Michael O'Connor

The Etiquette Advantage in Business: Personal Skills for Professional Success
by Peggy Post and Peter Post

Difficult Conversations
by Douglas Stone, Bruce Patton, and Sheila Heen

The Career Survival Guide
by Brian O'Connell

Overturning career roadblocks

Figuring out what went wrong 98
When you don't know what you did

Classic career mistakes 100
Patterns to avoid

Owning up to mistakes 102
Ways to fix your missteps

Communication blunders 104
Watch what you say and how you say it

Poor writing 106
The best letters, memos, and e-mails

E-mail snafus 108
It's so easy to do it wrong

The imperative to change 110
Change is in the air

Now what do I do? 112
Answers to common questions

figuring out what went wrong

How do you know when you've slipped up?

If you are continuously coming up against roadblocks in your career, it is incumbent upon you to figure out why you are having trouble advancing. Something is causing a problem. Like a good doctor, your first step is to diagnose your situation. The following tips are diagnostic tools:

Ask for feedback The best kind is 360-degree feedback; that is, collective information from bosses, peers, and subordinates. Many executive development programs have 360-degree diagnostic programs, specific instruments for getting people feedback from multiple layers in their organizations. While you may not have access to such a program, you can still seek insights about your behavior from people that encircle you. You might, for example, schedule conversations with two or three people in your workplace. Explain that you want to move up in your career and ask if they have insights into things that might be hampering you. When you ask senior people the same question, ask them if they have any ideas about how you can overcome these roadblocks. Be sure to thank everyone you talk to for their candor and time!

Measuring your behavior against others Look at the behavior of others in your organization: How do they deal with those issues that are challenging you? For example, if you have trouble getting your sales reports in on time, find out how the best performers in your department handle their sales reports. Perhaps they file weekly rather than monthly reports. Learn how others perform top-quality work and copy them.

Seeking professional help

If you are still receiving negative feedback from people in your organization, you would do well to find professional counseling. Talk to your doctor and ask for a referral for a therapist who can help you talk through your problems.

Meeting Savvy

In many companies, meetings are battlegrounds in which careers are made and lost. If you don't know the norms of your company regarding meetings, start paying close attention to them. Are meetings used for making—or just rubber-stamping—decisions? Sometimes the real meeting occurs—and a decision is made—behind the scenes before the official meeting takes place. People line up their coalitions beforehand, shutting out the uninitiated and unprepared. Observe how meetings work in your company. Note: If you are a woman, you may need to fight especially hard to be heard in meetings, but you must continue to participate and make sure your points are acknowledged. Meetings are also arenas in which lines of support and hierarchy are revealed. For this reason, where you sit—and where others sit—is hugely important. Try to position yourself near powerful people, without preempting the authority of the meeting organizer.

Handling Curveballs

In a meeting, questions may arise that you don't know the answer to, or situations may develop that take you off guard. If this happens, your goal is to slow things down and move the meeting on in a way that saves face for you and for the other attendees. Some strategies for doing this:

Repeat the question Many politicians use this time-honored tactic. If you are asked a question, first repeat it before giving your response—whether you know the answer or not. This helps you in several ways: First, it buys you some time to think. It also allows you to slightly rephrase the question into something you can answer. For example, if someone in the meeting exclaims, "I don't see how you think you can complete this project without any experience in this area," you could restate it as, "It sounds like I need to explain what I've learned in my past projects that will help me in this one." Finally, repeating the question shows the speaker that you are actively listening.

Ask a question If someone in a meeting says, "Tell me about the computer skills you could bring to this project," and you have few, you might reply, "It sounds like that's an important part of this project. Is a training course an option?" This is also a good strategy if you are asked a question and you want to clarify the questioner's underlying concern before responding.

State the obvious Just be honest. It's okay to say, "Good question! I need to think about it. Let me get back to you after the meeting." Try using humor, too.

classic career mistakes

What you do next
is critical

Most career mistakes are due to misjudgements that are usually fairly ingrained. While it can be hard to see these deep-rooted blind spots, it can be fairly easy to spot patterns of action that they leave in their wake. For example, some people consistently shrink when others disagree with their ideas. Rather than speaking up for themselves, they meekly let others disregard their ideas or take credit for them. In sharp contrast, some people yell and bang their fists on the table, making others wish that the loudmouth would grow up and learn how to express his ideas while controlling his anger.

Some misjudgements are worse than others. Some can even derail careers, while others are setbacks in an otherwise positive career trajectory. More important than the mistakes that you make, however, is figuring out the underlying causes of your misjudgements and correcting them. That determines long-term career success.

Career-related mistakes primarily come in seven varieties:

1. Not recognizing that jobs and careers have a "gamesmanship" quality

2. Misreading the environment of the organization of which you are a part

3. Letting others define your career and aspirations

4. Communicating with inappropriate language or tone

5. Not recognizing the need for change

6. Lacking empathy and being insensitive to how your actions impact others

7. Letting negative emotions such as greed overwhelm your good instincts

owning up to mistakes

When you create a problem in the workplace

Everyone makes mistakes. The trick is finding the best way to bounce back from them. That doesn't mean you should bury your mistake or deny your role in it. Far from it. In most cases, the best recourse is to step up to the plate and claim responsibility for your error. Why do this? Because it shows integrity and maturity—two traits that bosses most admire. To lessen the impact of your mistake, consider the following steps:

Tell your boss before anyone else does If you made a mistake that will prove harmful to your company, your department, or your boss, then tell your boss immediately. Do not let someone else tell her. Better she hears it from you. And if you take responsibility for the problem, she will be more likely to forgive you.

Stay poised Admit that you made a mistake and apologize, but don't put yourself down.

State what you have learned Mistakes can be great teachers. Tell your boss what you have learned from the mistake and how you will do better next time; give concrete examples of how you will handle the situation differently next time. If it is appropriate, ask for your boss's help in fixing the problem. Leave the conversation with direction in how to minimize the likelihood of the problem occurring again.

Use humor when you can Mistakes make everyone feel uncomfortable. Where it is appropriate try to use a little humor to leaven the situation. But be careful: This is not the time to appear flippant or casual.

FIRST PERSON   SUCCESS STORY

Turning a management blunder around

I was managing a department of five people and delegating work among them. One of my direct reports, Jake, repeatedly goaded me in different ways. He would complete half of an assignment and then ask what else was needed. He would borrow from his vacation days for the next year to take long trips. Rather than confront him, it just seemed easier for me to do Jake's work. Finally, I'd had enough. I got up the nerve to talk to a seasoned manager and asked for her feedback. She said Jake was playing with me and it was time to call him on it. She suggested I demand changes in his work and put it in writing. And so I did. I called Jake into my office and told him that he could no longer dump his work on me or anyone else and that I would hold him accountable if he did not turn in his work on time. And I put this all in a letter that I handed to him after our talk. Perhaps it was the fact that I put this in writing that did it. The point was that I had finally called his bluff and he started to pull his weight. Getting the right feedback saved me from a miserable management experience.

—Trisha L., Boston, MA

communication blunders

How you talk and what you say are major elements in your success in the workplace. While there is great variety in what is acceptable in different organizations, there are some communication patterns that are sure to offend and undermine your career. The top communicating blunders are:

Swearing Even in a heated argument, using four-letter words is simply not acceptable. Ever.

Using qualifiers, such as "maybe," "possibly" The same goes with "um," "like," and "you know." These little words can, like, you know, possibly weaken your statements.

Slang Your choice of words is important. As a man, you may think calling women "gals" or "girls" is cute, but many women are likely to find this language condescending and offensive.

Using technical jargon While you may think it shows your knowledge of your field, it usually alienates those who are less knowledgeable (for example, senior management). Use the language of your field, certainly, but without overreliance on jargon.

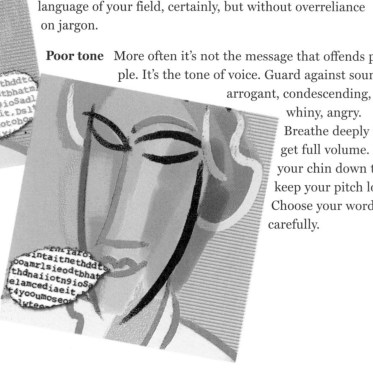

Poor tone More often it's not the message that offends people. It's the tone of voice. Guard against sounding arrogant, condescending, whiny, angry. Breathe deeply to get full volume. Keep your chin down to keep your pitch low. Choose your words carefully.

Common presentation problems

Presentations are a powerful vehicle to advance a career. If you have a well-prepared message, are articulate, have a confident and positive demeanor, and handle your audience well, you can gain great visibility in your organization, as well as ownership of the ideas or work you are discussing, and extend your influence across many people. That's the good news.

The bad news is that you may be making presentations in ways that diminish your credibility and authority. Not good for your career. Things to avoid:

Setting low expectations at the beginning Instead of telling your audience you haven't had time to prepare for the speech, or apologizing that your content is tedious and difficult to understand, begin by stating your credentials so they know you are someone worth listening to. Clearly state what you plan to talk about and how they will benefit from listening. Will they be able to make a better decision, clarify uncertainty, or put rumors to rest?

Diluting your message with weak language Throughout the main part of your presentation, avoid making disclaimers (e.g., "You may not believe this but . . ."), which set the audience up to discount whatever follows. Avoid qualifiers (e.g., "maybe," "a little," "possibly," "sometimes") and tag questions (e.g., "I believe we should proceed, don't you?"), which turn strong declarative statements into questions conveying uncertainty.

Taking away the value as you close You can appreciate the time your audience gave you, but don't apologize for the time you took, even if you ran over. Instead, remind them of your main points and how they will benefit by knowing them.

poor writing

Bring your skills up to par

Putting things in writing allows you to take ownership of your ideas, which brings recognition to your ideas. It serves as a record in time to mark your position (and cover your behind). Words on paper carry a more legitimate and powerful weight than the spoken word. But writing can also be misinterpreted or even distributed beyond the intended audience.

Think about these strategies for reducing your vulnerability before the next time you fire off a memo:

Before writing, consider nonwritten alternatives first It may be better to communicate verbally when you need immediate feedback, you want to see the reaction to your message, you need to negotiate, you need to persuade disinterested people, or you want to confirm agreements.

You don't want to write anything you wouldn't sign or want published in a newspaper; any disagreement after a decision has been made; any criticisms of management or their policies; gripes and grievances; or anything else that would be better shared in private.

When writing, predict the impact of your written word Consider how your message could be misinterpreted. Next, understand that no matter how carefully you write the message, your motives are usually transparent. Do you really want the boss to know you thought his decision was crazy? Unfortunately, those kinds of motives come across loud and clear through the tone of your writing.

Be aware of the vulnerability you create every time you add a name to the distribution list Before adding a name, ask yourself: Does this person need to know? What are my motives for including this person? Are they familiar enough with the subject so they won't misunderstand or misinterpret my information? Would I say the contents of my memo face-to-face? Is it politically appropriate for me to send it to them? What is the protocol of my organization regarding who gets what kind of information?

The smart memo

Memos are the workhorses of the business writing world. Their main purpose is to solve problems, either by informing someone about new info, such as policy changes or new hours, or by persuading someone to take action, such as attend a meeting or read a report.

In successful memos, the information is divided into these segments:

Heading segment This contains the reader's name, the sender's name, the date, and the subject. Make sure to address readers by their correct names and job titles. And be specific and concise in your subject line. For example, "New rule" is less helpful than "New rule about the water cooler."

Opening segment This gives the context (the event, circumstances, or background of the problem), a description of the problem, a specific assignment or task, and a summary of the purpose of the memo. Only include as much information here as decision-makers need to act.

Summary segment If your memo is longer than a page, consider writing a separate summary at the end that restates the key points and recommendations you've made.

Closing segment Make sure that you close with a courteous statement that makes clear the action you want the reader to take, as well as a deadline if appropriate.

You'll be less subject to misinterpretation if you:

- State the bottom line: what you want and why you are writing
- Organize the content around the readers' needs and anticipate their questions and reactions
- Do not assume their prior knowledge of the subject
- Use the active versus the passive voice
- Write like you talk
- Avoid euphemisms, doublespeak, and jargon

e-mail snafus

It may seem casual, but take it seriously

It's hard to imagine what the workplace would be like without e-mail. But because it's so prevalent, and because it's so quick and effortless to fire off, you can easily get into trouble with it. That's why it's smart not to put anything in an e-mail that you don't want forwarded to every person in the world. E-mail can be easily distributed, or cut and pasted out of context, and it also becomes a

permanent record on your company's server. Not only that, but your employer has the right to read your e-mails, so don't write anything you want to keep private. Also, if your company is being prosecuted, your e-mails can become part of the court record.

Keep things on the up-and-up with these savvy e-mail strategies:

Always respond and do so promptly People are quick to conclude that you don't care about them or their business if you don't respond to an e-mail within 24 hours. Even if you don't have time to act on their e-mail, let them know you received it and when they can expect a response. If you look at e-mail sporadically, use the auto-response to state that.

Be polite Always include a name when writing an e-mail, even if it is a reply to one. Always include a social close, such as "Regards, Ben." If you have time, include a salutation (e.g., "Hi there!"), possibly one sentence of human acknowledgment (e.g., "Hope you all are surviving the cold"). Salutations are especially important if you are e-mailing internationally or cross-culturally.

Keep your message brief Try to keep your e-mail to one page so that readers do not have to scroll down. At most, write a few paragraphs of several sentences each. Put the "bottom line" of your e-mail in the subject line. Deliver the main message in the lead paragraph.

Assess the tone of your message Choose your words carefully and imagine how your message will be received. Reread your message and ask yourself if the recipient can "mishear" any part of it. If you answer "yes," find a way to have a face-to-face conversation where you can deliver your message thoughtfully.

Check your spelling and grammar A misspelled e-mail looks unprofessional. Use capitalization and punctuation just as you would in any other document.

Be sparing with attachments Do not send attachments that restate what you wrote in your e-mail. Title the attached document in a way that will make it easy for the recipient to find once he downloads it.

Watch your formatting Be sure your e-mail is formatted to wrap your text after 70 characters to keep your e-mail from looking disjointed on the screen and in print.

Protect people's privacy While a lot of junk mail is forwarded to hundreds of people, you should not use this approach with work-related e-mail. Use blind carbon copy (BCC) for a professional e-mail to a group of people.

Use e-mail sparingly Don't irritate people by flooding them with FYI e-mails or forwarding junk.

Beware of IM!

More and more people are using instant messaging (IM) in the workplace these days. But be careful with it! Because IM is spontaneous, you may be tempted to type things to coworkers without thinking them through. Stick to business topics and use a professional tone. Every IM message is saved on the company server, even if you delete it on your PC. Not only can that cause you embarrassment, but your IMs can be used in a court of law. Finally: Don't IM friends at work—save it for home.

the imperative to change

Chances are, your department or organization is undergoing change. It may be the fundamental gut-wrenching type where colleagues are being laid off, and units closed. Or it may be incremental change where leadership is tinkering with products or service to customers.

Management gurus estimate that employees in organizations respond to change in thirds:

■ One third are resisters, refusing to acknowledge the need to change or complaining about proposed changes.

■ One third are fence-sitters, adapting a wait-and-see attitude and silently going about their work.

■ One third are supporters of the change, moving the changes forward.

In which third would you place yourself?

To meet the changing needs of organizations, leaders hire new bosses, often from outside the organization. The new boss talks with each person. Those who have an urge to get fired use phrases such as: "Gee, that's not in my job description." "We don't do it that way around here."

To drive the change down into the bowels of the organization, some bosses take drastic action. There is often a "public hanging," an employee fired because he was openly resisting the actions to turn around the organization.

If leaders in your organization are actively implementing change in your unit or department, mindfully situate yourself among the supporters for change. To do otherwise could be hazardous to your career health.

Ask the Experts

Our company is doing well, but our president has earmarked profits for overseas expansion. People are grumbling about how unfair these changes are. Is this a sign that I should look elsewhere?

You should assume that your president and the board of directors of your organization have determined that your company will be dramatically affected by globalization in the near future. Rather than wait for a drop in your company's market share, the executives decided to take positive forward-moving actions while your company is strong. Unfortunately, it sounds as if they have poorly communicated the reasons for the changes.

More than likely, the president has written and talked about his vision for the company. Get copies of these materials and read them carefully. Discuss their implications with your boss and colleagues. As you ask questions, be clear that you are seeking understanding, rather than resisting the changes. Once you understand the direction of the company, look for ways to support leading the changes, such as joining a task force.

My old boss was fired and replaced with someone outside the company who is holding individual conversations and asking people their perceptions and priorities for change. I'm worried that if I complain about my old boss, I'll seem disloyal. What do I say?

There should be three parts in your conversation with your new boss. First, be prepared to talk about the causes and possible solutions to the problems in your organization. Perhaps, for example, it takes too long to respond to customers in your unit. Explain your perception of the problem and one or two ways to handle it. Be clear with your new boss that you are in the one third of supporters of the change. You might volunteer for a new task or ask explicitly how you might help her with the new job. And finally, signal to your new boss that she now has your loyalty. If you go in to your new boss with an open-to-new-instructions attitude, you are likely to walk out of the office with new tasks. If you do, establish your dependability by performing the tasks exceptionally well and on time. Such an approach will make you a trustworthy member of your unit's team.

now what do I do?

I've been a project manager for several years. When I went to see
my boss to receive my latest marching orders, he wanted to try a
different approach. This is likely to increase the start-up phase of
the project and its costs. No one on the team is excited about trying
this new approach. How do I get my boss to see his mistake?

Instead of resisting his suggestions, say: "Tell me what is different
about this project and how you want the results to reflect those changes."
While people often rely on past methodologies to guide future ones, that
approach is sometimes untenable. Find out why your boss wants to
change your processes. His new goal may not be able to be reached
through the old processes. If you have serious concerns about the new
process, state them and ask how he'd suggest overcoming them.

Communicating with your team is your next step. Once you understand thoroughly why you should make the suggested changes, convey
this information with enthusiasm to your team. Not only do you want
them to understand the changes, you also need for them to support the
different approach.

For the past eight years, I have worked hard as an individual contributor. At last my boss is retiring and has recommended me for his
position. My boss's boss, however, has said that I must first serve in
an acting role. Since I have waited a long time for this promotion, I
don't know why I need to wait longer. What should I do?

You sound as if you feel entitled to this promotion. That is always a
mistake. It is highly possible that the top boss is reluctant to promote you
because she wants to see how you will perform in this new role. An attitude of energy and enthusiasm is vital if you want the promotion.

Accept the acting position with grace. Have a conversation with your
top boss about her vision for the role and how she will measure your performance. Set a time frame for the length of your acting appointment.

After your meeting, go to your desk and put in writing the parameters
of your conversation. This technique will assure both of you that you
share a vision for the work of your unit and how you will carry it out.

I heard from a colleague that I'm considered more of a tactician than a strategist. How can I turn that negative impression around?

Taking positive action in the face of criticism, rather than trying to defend yourself with words, is the easiest way to correct a colleague's negative impression of you and your work. Start by setting aside at least two hours on your calendar every week to engage in a range of activities, from analyzing economic forecasts to reading your industry's most popular journal. These activities will help make you a better strategist, and once this kind of planning becomes second nature to you, colleagues will begin to notice your positive actions, and their impression of you is apt to change quickly.

Helpful Resources

WEB SITES

Fortune magazine
www.fortune.com/careers
This specific site is part of *Fortune* magazine and focuses on career-related issues, including an online "Ask Annie" column.

AdvancingWomen.com
www.advancingwomen.com/workplace.html
This site focuses on helping women around traditional choke points in their careers so they can advance to the highest level of their capabilities.

BOOKS

Nice Girls Don't Get the Corner Office: 101 Unconscious Mistakes Women Make That Sabotage Their Careers
by Lois Frankel

Emotional Intelligence
by Daniel Goleman

Working with Emotional Intelligence
by Daniel Goleman

Building strategic relationships

The importance of allies 116
No one makes it alone

Formal mentors 118
How to prepare yourself to be a protégé

Group mentoring 120
The best relationships are balanced with give-and-take

Productive working relationships 122
Good working relationships are your career catalyst

Assessing your network 124
Take stock of who's in, who's not, and who should be

Professional associations 126
Gain knowledge and expand your network

Nurturing your network 128
Creating breadth and depth

Now what do I do? 130
Answers to common questions

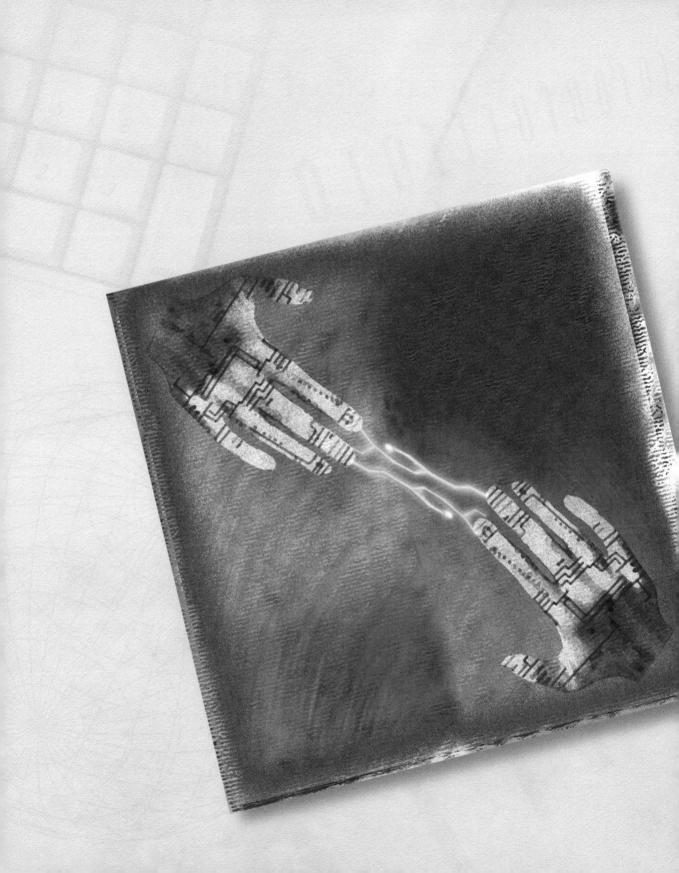

the importance of allies

No successful career happens without the help of others, especially those who have been down the same road you are attempting to travel. That's why it is imperative that you take it upon yourself to seek career advice from senior, wiser people in your field.

Who do you turn to? Start with former colleagues who have moved ahead faster than you on the corporate ladder. Or consider asking a former boss with whom you had a productive working relationship. Sometimes mentoring evolves after an informational interview, especially if you feel an affinity or chemistry between the two of you. When asking for someone to be your mentor, flattery will

go a long way; you might try couching your request this way: "I've been so impressed with the progress you've made at XYZ company recently, and I'm wondering if you might be able to assist me with my own career goals?"

In time and with time invested, your relationship will grow. Any relationship needs to be nurtured. So be sure to give back. Your mentor may need your opinion on something from time to time. What is the point of succeeding if there is no one there who understands how well you both did and how hard you worked for it?

What should I look for in a mentor?

As with any other kind of relationship, one of the important things you should look for when seeking a mentor is chemistry. You really want to find a mentor you feel comfortable talking to and who you think can connect with your career concerns. On top of that, you should look for a mentor who:

- **Is respected and respects others, too** The goal is to find a mentor who is well established in his field and has clout and connections you can make use of.

- **Believes in you** A mentor who has any doubts about you isn't going to make you feel any better about a sticky career situation; your mentor should be your champion and should want you to get ahead because he really thinks you are talented and capable.

- **Is accessible** While e-mail and phone calls are fine, ideally you should be able to meet up with your mentor in person from time to time.

- **Holds you accountable** A good mentor will not allow you to dismiss his advice and will get tough with you when necessary about your career goals or your career action plan.

- **Has a positive attitude** A mentor who has a bleak outlook on your talents or your industry is not going to instill in you the confidence and optimism you need to make great career leaps.

- **Is discreet** Anything you tell your mentor should be held in strictest confidence, and you should never worry that your most private career thoughts will leak into the public sphere and damage your career.

formal mentors

Company-fostered support

In the workplace, mentoring is a supportive relationship between a more experienced employee and a less experienced one. In formal mentoring programs, HR or management matches mentors with promising young employees. Senior staff gives organization-specific career advice and acts as advocates for its protégés. The advantage of a formal mentoring program is that someone in authority takes responsibility for making a good match; the disadvantage is that sometimes the relationship lacks chemistry.

If your workplace offers a formal mentoring program, gather information about it and decide if it's for you. Formal mentors can provide two main kinds of support. The first kind is career-related advice or help. For example, a mentor may recommend you for a special task force or a job that she knows will stretch and enrich your skills or career. Or your mentor may sponsor you for a special training program.

The second function of a mentor can be to provide encouragement and support. In this case, your mentor may be able to act as a reliable sounding board who will listen to you during tough times. The strongest mentor-mentee relationships include both career-related and emotional support.

Ask the Experts

I'm hesitant to look for a mentor because I feel like I would be asking for too much help. What does the mentor get out of it?

Being a mentor is a good business strategy for ambitious managers because it shows that they care about talent development, or tapping and developing young talent to fit the company's changing needs. In many cases, raises and promotions for senior management are tied into their success at mentoring and nurturing talent. In this sense, the mentoring relationship is a win-win situation for everyone.

How much more senior than I should my mentor be?

Usually a mentor is about three to four rungs up the career ladder from you. Although in **step-ahead mentoring**, your mentor may only be one rung up and may occupy a position that might be considered a good next career step for you. Sometimes organizations assign step-ahead mentors to help new employees learn the ropes of the company, but you can also seek them out on your own. If you do have this kind of mentor, tread carefully, since he may rightfully view you as a competitor for his job.

group mentoring

There is strength in numbers

Group mentoring can be a great idea when employees would benefit from being mentored by a variety of people with different job responsibilities. In this, several people with approximately the same status and level of experience form a collective and provide career advice and emotional support for one another. The collective knowledge in such groups creates a complex web of relationships that can help you advance.

As with any type of mentoring relationship, the **rule of reciprocity** is paramount here. Even if you think you don't have much helpful advice to offer the people in your mentoring group, make sure that you're not always "taking" from the group. Not sure how you can reciprocate? Ask.

Ask the Experts

How do I set up a mentoring circle?

If you think **mentoring circles** would work well at your company, consider describing the idea to HR and your boss and getting their support, or forming an advocacy group to establish mentoring circles. Or you might lobby for creating a **peer-mentoring** program if that would suit your organization better. In both cases, not only will you get the mentoring you need, you'll also stand out in management's eyes for having promoted a culture of support and sharing in your organization.

Mentoring circles

These days, savvy corporations are experimenting with mentoring circles, which are formally recognized groups of employees that meet regularly with a senior staff member. Their purpose is to provide career advice and support to junior employees through conversations on specific topics with senior staff and peers. The senior staff member acts as a motivator by fielding questions and facilitating answers.

Mentoring circles can be the perfect solution for organizations that do not have a formal mentoring program because of a perceived lack of mentors—such as at companies that have more junior than senior staff. One clear advantage to mentoring circles is that these groups give mentees access to the advice and knowledge of peers as well as managers. These circles are also time-efficient for busy executives because they allow them to mentor multiple people at once.

Don't overlook your colleagues

In peer mentoring, employees who have approximately the same level of experience, status, and job responsibilities form mentoring relationships with each other. This kind of mentoring is probably one of the easiest mentoring relationships to form since it's between equals.

productive working relationships

Reciprocity, respect, rapport, and trust are key

Productive working relationships are the real key to your career success. Sure, your knowledge and skills may get you a job or special assignment, but your career will advance faster if people enjoy working with you. Keep in mind that managing yourself and your relationships with others in an organization is a complex and multidimensional process. When in doubt, just remember that your goal is to develop strong working relationships with higher-ups, peers, and subordinates.

There are four critical elements to developing strong professional relationships: reciprocity, respect, rapport, and trust. Without these, your working relationships are likely to be problematic.

Reciprocity This means that there must be give-and-take in a relationship. While you don't need to go as far as keeping a list of who has done what for you, do be mindful of what you ask for—and give. (See pages 84–85 for more.)

Respect This is something that everyone—regardless of his role in an organization, salary, or education—deserves. Every person deserves to be treated courteously. (See pages 36–42.)

Rapport This means having harmonious relations with colleagues, which is facilitated by understanding the norms of your workplace. Rapport also requires "chemistry," that subtle sense of being in tune with coworkers and being able to communicate easily and effectively.

Trust This is something that must be earned. People learn to trust you, for example, if you are asked to keep information confidential and you do. In turn, if you entrust someone with private information, you will be able to judge that person's trustworthiness based on whether the information gets into the office rumor mill or remains private. (See page 81.)

Forming alliances

Just as governments form alliances with other governments around the world to extend their influence, so too do you need to develop allies: people who support and extend your influence. An **ally** can come in handy by convincing other people of the merit of an idea you have. Or when a project is being planned, an ally may suggest you be brought on to the team.

Use the chart below to list your current allies and figure out others with whom you would like to be connected. Then write down action steps that you will take to fill the gap in your strategic alliances. This could mean scheduling a meeting, taking a potential ally out to lunch, trying to get assigned to a project with a potential ally—anything that will build connections between you.

Inside My Organization

	Who knows about my work?	Who needs to know about my work?
Above me		
My peers		
Below me		

Outside My Organization

	Who knows about my work?	Who needs to know about my work?
Leaders		

Action plan: what I will do to fill these gaps

_____

_____

_____

assessing your network

Reflect on who's in your web of contacts

Networking, or connecting with people through other people, is a fundamental building block of a successful career and can serve multiple purposes. If you are job-hunting, for example, you may be seeking hard-to-find information about a privately owned organization. With a well-honed, expansive network, you'll have a better chance of finding this info. Your network can also connect you—or colleagues you want to help—to great job openings, joint project opportunities, and people you can add to your personal board of directors. (See page 28.)

As part of the process of optimizing your career, you need to take a strategic approach to expanding your existing network. But a good network isn't just about breadth—it's about depth, too. You need to focus not just on expanding your network to include contacts who can help you reach your next career goal, but also on deepening ties with your most crucial contacts.

Before you can take this kind of strategic approach to your network, you first need to have an accurate assessment of it. This takes some time and reflection. The exercise on the next page can help you analyze your current network and find the gaps, then come up with a plan to close them.

As you start to take stock of your network, you may find yourself wondering exactly who's in and who's out. The basic rule: Your network only includes people who know you and your work. You may, for example, have met the president of your organization, but unless you can comfortably pick up the phone and talk to her, you should not consider her part of your network.

Your network: present and future

Step 1 Start by listing people you know in the categories below. And let yourself free-associate: One name may lead to another in a different category, which may remind you of a recent training course and a few more names. Mark next to the name whether the person is a close or distant connection. For example, a colleague who shares your profession and with whom you work regularly would be a close professional associate, whereas a professional-school classmate from a decade ago would probably be a distant professional associate. After spending a good half hour or so on this, set it aside for a day or two.

People you know

Your profession

Your industry

The organization that
currently employs you

Former employers

College and graduate school alumni

Professional associations

Social organizations or sports teams

Personal friendships

Religious organizations

Hobby-related groups

Neighborhood folks

Step 2 Review your lists and if any other people come to mind, add them. Then, in the context of your career goals over the next 18 months (see page 14), envision your ideal network. Do you need to add a significant number of contacts? In which categories? Can any current contacts lead you to these new ones? Do you need to reconnect with anyone from your past?

Step 3 Create a new list called "future network" with these new names and their contact info. Next to each name, outline steps for bringing this person into your network, such as calling or e-mailing, sending copies of your recent projects or presentations that they might find interesting, inviting them out to dinner or to an industry lecture—whatever would be the most efficient way of connecting with them.

professional associations

Going beyond membership

Think back to your school days. Like most students, you probably learned just as much outside of the classroom as inside. Whether you were on the debate team, ran track, or started a computer club, you no doubt picked up valuable knowledge and skills related to problem-solving, teamwork, and more.

In the same way, you can expand and enhance your skill sets and career connections by joining **professional associations**. These offer a variety of benefits, especially if you become actively involved and take on leadership roles. Although the specific advantages vary, most associations offer these three basic opportunities:

Professional-development programs and products Through conferences, educational programs, and publications, professional associations can help you stay on the cutting edge of your field. Just reading about the topics of a conference, for example, will give you clues about the hot areas of your field. You'll learn even more if you attend, and expand that exponentially if you prepare and make a presentation.

Career-enhancing connections A key benefit of joining professional associations is that they enable you to create strong professional relationships beyond your organization. To do this, you'll need to become actively involved in the association by volunteering for committee work or taking on leadership roles. This will also give you great opportunities to develop new skills; for example, if you're interested in event planning, volunteer to help organize the awards banquet for your association's next conference. Think strategically about the roles you take on, then squeeze as much knowledge from them as you can.

Recognition and awards Many professional associations recognize people for their outstanding contributions to the field, so it pays to be aware of these awards and put your work forward for consideration; such awards only enhance your visibility and respect in the field.

Ask the Experts

I know of at least a dozen professional associations related to my field. How do I figure out which are the best ones to join?

Since most professions have multiple associations, doing some research first is a must. Start online by searching professional associations in your field at sites like **www.rileyguide.com**. Once that's done, you'll be in a good position to talk with senior management in your organization about the professional associations they belong to and the benefits of each. Next, contact local branches of associations that interest you and find out where, when, and how often they meet, so that if you join more than one, their meetings won't conflict. If you are still unsure, try attending the annual conferences of several organizations to see which ones feel like the best fit for you.

Over the past year I've attended three or four meetings of my association, as well as the annual conference. I've met a lot of people, but haven't really connected with anyone. What should I do now?

It's not enough to just go to the meetings—you need to get involved. At the next association meeting, introduce yourself to someone in a position of authority, explain your background briefly, and then ask for advice about options for getting actively involved in the organization. Since most professional associations run largely on volunteer manpower, you're likely to get an enthusiastic response, and you'll probably be directed toward several committees that could make use of your skills. Taking on active roles should go a long way toward helping you make deeper connections with other members of the association.

nurturing your network

Take care of it, and it will take care of you

Like plants, networks are organic: If you nurture them and feed them regularly, they will grow and flourish, but without attention, they will quickly wither and die. Caring for your network takes considerable planning and maintenance; you want to cultivate existing contacts while also adding new ones.

Here are some other tips for creating and maintaining a healthy network:

Make it multidimensional Your goal should be to have diversified networks: webs of connections within and across your profession, industry, and social sphere. For example, if you're a a legal expert in the high-tech industry, connect with others like you, but also with lawyers and high-tech professionals at legal firms, ad firms, and in social groups like your book club or church.

Keep tabs on your network Organize and cross-reference your contacts by field, position, and type. Also note any specialized career knowledge they have, when and where you met them, any personal information you've collected, and any important meetings or events you've attended with them.

Always be prepared In many ways, managing your network is a mind-set that translates into useful behaviors like always carrying your business cards, preparing small-talk topics to break the ice with strangers, and perfecting methods for meeting new people and remembering their names.

Nurture your connections Go the extra mile to nurture relationships with your contacts. Send relevant articles, send notes to congratulate them on career milestones, and meet up periodically.

Reciprocate Remember that networks go both ways. When other people contact you as part of their own strategic networking, go out of your way to help them and provide additional resources. You never know how they might help you down the road.

Ask the Experts

I feel like I've hit a brick wall in my networking efforts at work. Where else can I make good business contacts?

Many successful businesspeople make contacts outside of work that help them progress in their designated careers. Some venues you might try:

The playing field Yes, you can learn to play golf, but other types of sporting events can be just as useful. You might just hear about a great opening in your company while seated next to the VP at your son's Little League game.

The charity circuit Community involvement via your company's volunteer program not only improves your company's reputation, it can also enhance your own sense of worth and connect you with other professionals who volunteer.

The classroom Furthering your education can bring you into contact with executives in other firms while you enhance your job skills, too.

The Social Scene Gallery openings, dinner parties, chance meetings on trips—all are opportunities to exchange business cards and gather information.

FIRST PERSON SUCCESS STORY

Company alumni network saves the day

A few years ago I was working for an Internet start-up, and like many others during that period, our company eventually went under. After we were laid off, our HR director created a private online forum at Yahoo!Groups and invited all 25 former employees to join up and help each other with their job searches. We networked like mad, sharing contacts, advice, frustrations, and successes as many of us went on to get new jobs in more stable industries. Instead of having the power of just one network—my own—I was able to take advantage of the networks of all 25 people, and got a great new job via one of these new contacts. Though the group isn't as active as it once was, many of us "alumni" still check in every few weeks and post contacts and news that might be helpful to former coworkers.

—Alison L., Portland, OR

now what do I do?

Answers to common questions

I'm in my mid 20s and people tell me I look as if I just graduated from high school. When I go to professional meetings, no one takes me seriously since they assume I'm still in school. Most top-level executives won't even talk to me. What can I do?

There are several strategies you can try here. First, it's important that you dress to signal that you are a serious professional. Make sure your hairstyle is neat and always wear professional-looking clothes, rather than casual or hip ones. Experts also say you should dress for the job you want to have, or the next job up the ladder—not the one you have now. Observe business etiquette about arriving on time, greeting people, and handing out your business card, then follow suit. Last and most important, read newspapers and journals relevant to your field so you will sound like the committed professional that you are. (If you don't feel confident speaking this way, take some confidence-boosting or public speaking courses.) When you join small groups of people, add value to the conversation by talking about what you have read and insights that you have gained. In formal settings, ask savvy questions of the speakers, which will give you visibility and credibility. If you take on tasks and do an exceptional job in a professional way, people will soon seek you out for your professional input.

There is a successful VP in my company whom I admire and respect. We don't have a formal mentoring program at my company. Can I still ask her to be my mentor? How?

If you do not have a formal mentoring program, there is danger of creating an uncomfortable situation if you ask someone directly to be your mentor—especially if she is a high-ranking person who doesn't want to take on the responsibility. An alternative approach is to work on strengthening your relationship with her. Ask her career-related questions. To reciprocate, give her copies of articles that you believe she would find useful (but don't overdo it). By building a strong relationship over time and reciprocating her attention, it's possible that your relationship will naturally evolve into a mentoring one.

I have a colleague who joined an online networking group. How do they work?

The practice of taking personal networking online is called **hypernetworking**. Free sites such as **Tribe.net** and **Friendster.com** are largely social networking sites, while **Spoke.com**, **Ryze.com**, and **LinkedIn.com** are business networking sites.

While these last three sites share a common purpose, they work quite differently. Spoke, for example, uses data from your e-mail and other information systems to discover your existing relationships and build a private, secure relationship network for you. You do not manually enter additional data; rather, Spoke continually indexes any new relationship information you add as you go about your day, visiting sites and e-mailing friends and associates.

Most important, before you sign up for any of these communities, be sure to read the privacy and user agreements thoroughly, and talk to as many others as you can about their experiences on them. Note that of the three business networking sites mentioned here, LinkedIn has received the most positive reviews.

Helpful Resources

WEB SITES

LinkedIn.com
www.linkedin.com
This is considered the hottest online networking site.

VolunteerMatch
www.volunteermatch.org
Connects volunteers to opportunities in their area.

BOOKS

The Five Patterns of Extraordinary Careers: The Guide for Achieving Success and Satisfaction
by James M. Citrin and Richard A. Smith

The Practical Coach: Management Skills for Everyday Life
by Paula J. Caproni

The Smart Woman's Guide to Career Success
by Janet Hawter

CHAPTER 7

Moving up

Internal opportunities 134
Your next move may be down the hall

Getting project work 136
Great career building blocks

Getting a raise 138
Be ready to state your case

Asking for a promotion 140
A little preparation goes a long way

Negotiating for yourself 142
Negotiating tips

Interviewing in another department 144
Don't get derailed when you have the inside track

Gendered expectations 146
Know the rules to get what you deserve

Weighing a promotion 148
Do you really want the job?

Now what do I do? 150
Answers to common questions

internal opportunities

You're working for a great company and you are very happy in your job. Now all you have to do is keep cranking out good work, and you'll automatically move up the promotional ladder, right? Maybe . . . and maybe not. There's more to getting ahead than simply doing a good job. You need to market yourself, yes, even to the company you already work for. That means you need to be aware of what it takes to grow your career at your company. In most cases, it is a combination of visibility, luck, and determination.

Start by researching what opportunities are available in your company and how people have taken advantage of them in the past.

■ Build your information pipeline. Target people who are good sources of information and/or in positions to make things happen (e.g., your boss, coworkers, HR, other departmental managers, or industry associates). Take note of who gets written up in the company newsletter and why, who gets assigned to high-visibility teams, or who is talked about by other people. That's who you want to talk to.

■ Ask your sources what they're working on, challenges they're facing, frustrations they have, or what they'd like to tackle. Find out what's in the pipeline before projects, teams, jobs, or task forces have been staffed. These conversations can often help you identify ways to get involved or snag an internal job opening.

■ If something you hear strikes you as promising or necessary for your career development, make it clear that you are seeking opportunities to make an impact in the company. Briefly tell them about the transferable skills and experience you'd bring to any project or job they may have open in the future.

■ Ask permission to stay in touch and then be diligent about doing so.

How to get noticed

Company insiders can't offer you that new project you're interested in if they don't know your name. Consider these ideas for making a name for yourself across the organization:

Get involved in other departments Volunteer to serve on cross-departmental committees or to make presentations to other departments. Help plan company parties or outings.

Write for the company newsletter Write up brief descriptions of interesting projects your department is working on. Submit a profile on an "unsung hero" in your department, or personal tidbits on receiving your master's degree or biking to raise money for cancer. And put your name in the byline.

Speak up at meetings Meetings are a big proving ground inside organizations. Everyone notices who talks and who doesn't and whose opinion prevails. So speak up! For nervous types, this could mean preparing something in advance or offering to cover an agenda point. Speak audibly, enunciate, and minimize the use of qualifiers (words like "maybe," "possibly," "could") that dilute the impact of your comments.

Don't eat at your desk No matter how much work you have, don't eat lunch alone. Go to the company cafeteria or eat lunch with colleagues. It's a great opportunity to network and trade company news. Rather than eating at your desk, make a point of having lunch once a week with someone from another department. Ask him about the challenges facing him, his department, and the company, and any opportunities he foresees.

Attend social functions You may find company holiday parties and golf tournaments boring and stiff, but these events may be your only chance to interact informally with senior staff from other departments.

Use information to connect with people If you read a newspaper article or find a Web site that a colleague may find useful, send a copy or forward the link. This thoughtful touch may open doors for you.

getting project work

Your next big opportunity
may not be a job

Being able to recognize and grab career opportunities often requires changing your perspective. For example, it may mean realizing that your next great job opportunity is just down the hall. It may also mean expanding your concept of the term "job," because in fact your next job may actually be a project or assignment, like helming a task force or filling a position temporarily.

Like a great job, a great project can be an excellent résumé builder if you choose one that:

Provides visibility Working on this project should expose you to key people in the organization—people who can further your career opportunities.

Adds to your network Colleagues on this project should be people you want to add to your "network" of contacts.

Develops new skills The new skills and knowledge you will pick up should expand your options for future jobs and projects.

Builds your value The project should play a key role in meeting company goals, and provide you with the opportunity to make an important contribution.

Once you've identified such a project, you need to get assigned to it. How? Market yourself! Whether you are writing an e-mail to the project leader or interviewing with him, ask the following:

- What needs does the project have?
- What obstacles are they facing?
- How are they falling short of their goals?

Next, convey what you can bring to the project—your skills, your knowledge, and your networks. Focus in particular on what you uniquely offer.

Finally, link their needs to your skills and specify how the project will benefit from using you.

Ask the Experts

I was assigned to head up our department's communication task force, and I'm feeling overwhelmed. Can I delegate some of the work? If so, how do I do it?

It's common for employees who are put in new positions of responsibility to feel they should do it all themselves because they think they have to prove themselves, or because they think only they know the subject matter well enough to do the work. Don't fall

into this trap, which can lead you to take on too much and make mistakes. Instead, delegate various tasks to team members based on their knowledge, skills, and willingness. Clearly state your expectations and the requirements of the project, and set deadlines for check-ins and completion. Then empower teammates by asking for their ideas about how they think they can best accomplish the task, and ask them to create an action plan. Make sure they know what resources are available to help them do the job, and meet with them regularly to assess their progress. When the task is done, evaluate their work and give constructive feedback. By following these steps, you'll complete the project and you'll get a head start on learning important management skills that can serve you well later on.

getting a raise

Yͮou have been doing good work and your job reviews reflect your efforts. Moreover, you've also put in extra time on two projects that were critical to a new product launch. Surely you're due for a raise. You haven't had one in a year, meaning the value of your salary has gone down. A cost-of-living increase of 3 percent, which keeps pace with inflation, is not a raise; it just keeps you dead even. No doubt your boss will give you a raise when he can.

But in thinking like this, you're expecting him to be aware of all that you do and to constantly fight for more money for you. Most likely, this won't happen, for one very important reason: Your boss gets rewarded for controlling costs, not increasing them.

To increase the likelihood that you'll get a "yes":

■ Rather than trying to get an exception made, learn everything you can about your organization's compensation system by reading employee manuals or talking to people in HR. You want to uncover salary ranges and know the constraints your boss may be under.

■ Don't expect to "win" a raise after one interaction with the boss. View your quest as a campaign over time.

■ Don't say you need a raise . . . show how you deserve a raise. Use all the documentation you've collected in preparing for a job review.

When to ask for a raise

■ When you have learned (through networking, reading salary reports on the Web, or interviewing) that you are being underpaid.

■ When you have taken on more job responsibilities.

Ask the Experts

I have a performance appraisal coming up in four months. Should I just wait to ask for a raise then?

No, it may be too late by then. That's because many organizations link salary increases with the performance appraisal process. Once your boss says, "Thanks for all your work; here's a 4 percent raise," he's already made up his mind and distributed limited resources across everyone in the department. Get ahead of him by asking for a raise well before the appraisal process. At best, he'll now be considering your request separately from his other employees, and at the least, you'll be "planting seeds" in his mind as he enters appraisal time.

I'm embarrassed to ask for a raise. For some reason it makes me feel like I'm begging.

Don't beg, sell. Think of asking for a raise as pitching a proposal to a prospective customer. Tell him how the company has benefited from your contributions. Build your case with specific examples. Write out your points and practice them out loud or with a friend. As with any skill, the more often you ask, the better you'll get!

I asked my boss for a raise and she said, "Let me think about it." It's been a week. Now what?

Whenever you ask for a raise, have a "plan B" that you'll act on if you don't get it. First, don't give up just yet. She may really need to think about it. Give her another week and then bring it up again, asking what else you can do to make it happen. If you do get a "no":

Ask, "What do I need to do to earn a raise?" Map out specific job responsibilities you have to take on, or areas you need to strengthen. Ask, "When will we talk about this again? Six months?" to lock in a firm next step.

Negotiate for something the boss can give you. She may not be able to increase your salary, but she may be able to give you Friday afternoons off or a PC for at-home work.

Smile, thank her, and start a job search.

asking for a promotion

Moving up in your department

You know you're ready for a promotion when your actual job duties far exceed your current job description, when you've outgrown your current job and need new challenges, or when the promotion will take you where you want to go next on your career path within your current department.

You also know you're ready for a promotion when you've considered how your responsibilities would be different after the promotion and you're comfortable with what that would mean. You should feel confident that the promotion will make you happy, that you are ready to stretch yourself in a new role, and that you will have access to resources (e.g., training, upper management support, or staff) you will need to be successful in the job. If you're a proven contributor, then go for it. But don't ask for a promotion because you feel you deserve it or they "owe" it to you. Promotions and raises often aren't about fairness or rewarding *past* performance. They're about what management anticipates you'll do for the organization in the *future*.

But first, you need to prepare just as you would prepare for a job interview, even though it's with your current boss. Learn all you can about the new job's required skills and responsibilities.

Make it easy for your boss to say "yes":

■ Pick the right time to meet about it. Don't ask for a promotion right after fourth-quarter numbers come in surprisingly low or the company loses a major client.

■ Schedule an appointment and let the boss know in advance what you want to talk about. Give her your materials (résumé, proposed job description) ahead of time so she can review them.

■ Focus on how the organization will benefit with you in this job and how your boss's goals will be better addressed—in short, what's in it for them.

■ Prepare to be asked: Can you do the job? Will it impact current work processes and people if you move? Who is going to handle your old job?

Preparing for a promotion

If you feel you deserve a promotion, your boss may ask you why you think so, so prepare ahead of time for this meeting by doing the following:

Collect proof of your accomplishments (See page 12 on creating a career portfolio.) Keep a folder on your computer and one in your desk drawer containing anything that documents your great work:

- "job well done" e-mails
- certificates of achievement and diplomas
- performance appraisals
- awards and plaques
- articles in company newsletters about your work

Also consider creating a portfolio using a three-ring binder and acetate sleeves.

Craft success stories Make an impression during a promotion meeting by sharing "success stories" of recent achievements. Create and memorize five or six stories, each two minutes long and highlighting a different skill. Use the **START** format:

S What was the **Situation**? Where and when did your action take place?

T What was the **Trouble**? What obstacles or problems called for your action?

A What **Action** did you take?

R What were the **Results** or outcomes? Can you quantify those results?

T What are the **Transferable** skills you used that you can bring to this job?

Quantify your successes To prove that these outcomes really occurred and benefited the company, quantify (provide a numeric measure of) the outcomes. "We were able to complete five more projects per month" sounds better than "We could get more work done." Employers love to hear how you helped them save or make money, so ask yourself, "How did my action help the bottom line?" You can also try showing how you improved productivity (through minimizing errors, waste, or duplication, or maximizing resources) or image (in the eyes of customers, shareholders, Wall Street, other departments).

negotiating for yourself

When it comes to negotiating raises and promotions, the hard truth is that the failure to do so can affect your entire career. Avoiding or flubbing a single negotiation can hamper your earning power for the rest of your career by anchoring your salary at a lower figure. And not requesting that promotion may take the shine off your résumé, making it look like you've been in the same job for years. True, your responsibilities may have increased, but without that visible job-title change, many potential employers will give you a pass.

To successfully negotiate a raise or promotion, follow these steps during the meeting:

Remind your boss of your value Address the value you have already brought to the company and the future value you'll bring before mentioning a raise or promotion. For example, "In the last year alone, I brought in over $200,000 in new contracts, and I also developed and implemented a new training program that resulted in . . ."

Make your request Now you can move on to asking for what you want and explaining how this change will benefit the company. "I think that as a department manager, I can bring in even more revenue because I will be able to train my direct reports in my selling skills."

Keep it short and sweet Stay focused on your priorities and keep it brief. Don't be tempted to continue justifying or explaining your request, and avoid becoming defensive or self-effacing ("I know it may seem I don't really deserve this promotion yet, but . . ."). The point is to come across as confident, realistic, and rational.

Be patient At this point, your boss will likely comment on your request, but don't expect an immediate decision; he will probably need to check with several people.

FIRST PERSON SUCCESS STORY

Making a case for myself

After two years of serving in tech support, I was ready to move into a marketing position. The marketing department was always in a frenzy to meet deadlines, so I knew the only way I'd get a "yes" from my boss was to make it as easy as possible for him. I did the usual homework, but two strategies really made the difference. First, I put everything in writing: I wrote up a brief that included what I wanted and why my track record worked for this position. Second, I made sure I put my contributions in terms of how I'd helped him provide tech support for the entire marketing team. I didn't just talk about how I'd surpassed my goals, but about how I'd helped him surpass his goals. He agreed to my request, and I got my promotion and raise.

—Devorah M., Winchester, MA

Brush up on your negotiation skills

There are several organizations that teach courses or offer seminars on negotiating. Here are just a few:

■ Harvard University Law School offers a semester-long course (**www.law.harvard.edu/programs**) and shorter programs (**www.pon.execseminars.com**).

■ Simmons School of Management (SOM) has a negotiation program for women. Check out **www.simmons.edu/som/executive**.

■ The American Management Association (AMA) offers short courses on negotiating. Learn more at **www.amanet.org/seminars**.

interviewing in another department

You'll have different hurdles to clear

Through networking internally or reviewing the job section of your company's Web site, you've identified a great new job in another department in your company. Do you tell your current boss about it or wait? Should you tell your coworkers?

All of these questions require you to have a good sense of your company's culture (see page 34) and its internal hiring policies and practices. If there is no policy to guide you, consider talking confidentially to a colleague who made an internal move to find out how she did it.

If you apply and are called for an interview for the new position, don't assume, even if you know the new boss, that you can both relax during the interview. In fact, it is in your best interest that this interview follow the same interview process as with outside candidates. Why? Because you want a chance to provide information about yourself and answer the new boss's concerns without any reliance on previous working knowledge about you—knowledge that may even be inaccurate. And just like in any other interview, you need to prepare to answer all questions, especially those that deal with preconceived ideas about your work history and its effect on the present job. Prevent them from pigeonholing you in your current capacity by addressing this issue head-on. For example, "I understand that the organization may see me as a sales rep, but here's what I've done to prepare to step into a managerial role . . ."

Once the issue of your reputation has been addressed, try to find out what this potential new boss needs. If he wants someone who can get up to speed quickly, focus on your solid knowledge of the company, product, or customers. But if he wants new ideas, your insider status and familiarity with "business as usual" at your company may work against you. Instead, share success stories (see page 141) that demonstrate innovative problem-solving and challenging the status quo.

Ask the Experts

When do I tell my current boss that I want to interview for another job?

No boss wants to be the last to learn that you're leaving, even more so if you are leaving for another department in the company. Not being informed makes your boss look bad and that can hurt you later as you move up the corporate ladder. Most companies have procedures for handling this situation, so talk to HR about your interest in an open position and find out how to proceed. Usually, these procedures aim to retain good employees by supporting their efforts to advance in the company, while preventing managers from "raiding" one another's employees. For example, you may have to get your current manager's sign-off.

A good first step is to tell your current manager about this new job opening elsewhere in the company. Ideally, your boss is already familiar with your career goals and will be supportive. It's in most bosses' best interests to help foster the career development of their employees. Only if you know for sure that his reaction will be to block your effort, or at least make your life miserable, should you wait until you have a job offer in hand.

I competed for a job against an external candidate who eventually got the job. I feel like the company just went through the motions with me but didn't really see me as a contender. I am really demoralized. What now?

Use this as a valuable experience that can provide you with vital career information. Start by asking HR or the other manager for feedback on why you didn't get the job. Should you get more training? Which projects would prepare you for the next job? And look on the bright side: You did gain good visibility and showed a willingness to take on new responsibilities.

gendered expectations

To get promoted you have to know what's valued

If you ask most bosses what their main criterion is for promoting someone, chances are they would say competence. That's the ability to get things done using both your well-honed skills and your technical knowledge about the job. While competence may seem like a fairly objective criterion, the truth is that the idea of competence can often look different depending on whether you're a man or a woman.

Male employees usually find it easy to demonstrate competence, since the behaviors that signal competence are considered "what guys do" in our society: making decisions unilaterally, taking charge, telling other people what to do, aggressively competing for resources, and promoting themselves and their good work to their bosses.

But if you try to visualize a woman demonstrating competence, you can easily see the "double bind" she faces: If she doesn't demonstrate aggressive behavior, her boss may not think she's assertive or tough enough—key attributes for landing plum assignments and moving up the career ladder. On the other hand, if she does perform with the same competence (that is, aggressive persistence) as her male colleagues, she may be seen as demanding, perfectionist, and controlling—all of which can be detrimental to her career. This differing of criteria based on gender is called gendered expectations.

Gendered expectations about competence can impact a woman's career in many ways. To counter it, you first need to learn how your company's corporate culture works. How does senior management define competency? What does it value most in its managers? Are people skills denigrated at the expense of technical skills? Many of these values are not clearly articulated; you may have to tease them out by being extra-sensitive to your environment. Once you know what is expected, you can work to show your competency.

FIRST PERSON SUCCESS STORY

It's all about the bottom line

I'm a product manager at a printing company. In my most recent performance appraisal, my boss told me I needed to be more decisive. I was surprised by this and asked my boss for an example. He pointed out that I always ask others for input into decisions. Hearing that, I realized that my boss doesn't see the benefits of how I come to decisions through consensus, and instead he views me as being "afraid to make a decision on my own." I explained how my consensus-building conversations allow my units to share their best ideas with me so I can reach an optimal solution. I gave an example of how one team used another team's idea to reduce costs in their unit. I have also started writing short reports for my boss after each of my unit director meetings, explaining outcomes and how the organization has benefited from them. Last week, he called me into his office and said that he now sees the value of my way of reaching decisions, and has promised to make note of this in my next evaluation.

—**Kristina W., Nashville, TN**

Hidden expectations

Some companies have hidden expectations about diversity and about which kinds of employees should get promoted, and into which jobs. Be aware of management trying to pigeonhole you into a particular kind of job because it's "women's work" or because you belong to an ethnic group that they think excels at a certain kind of work. The same goes for people who are not usually considered "diverse"; for example, management may unconsciously promote more men into positions that require a lot of travel because they don't think of men as the primary caretakers in the family. If you think you are the target of such hidden expectations, make a point of asking for the work you want and demonstrating your unique skills and talents for doing that particular job.

weighing a promotion

You can say no

Being offered a promotion is an "offer you can't refuse"—isn't it? Not necessarily. Before you jump on a promotion, consider how it would affect your work/life balance (see Chapter 9) and ask yourself these questions:

■ **"Will this make me happy?"** If you already get great satisfaction from your current job, ask yourself if you would be equally rewarded by the new responsibilities being offered. Often a promotion entails less time doing actual work (writing code, analyzing data, balancing budgets) and more time managing people. If this shift isn't appealing, decline the offer. You probably won't be happy, and your work will reflect it.

■ **"Am I ready to stretch myself?"** Before turning down a promotion because you dread the added responsibilities, realize that the only way to grow is to get out of your comfort zone. You may feel unqualified now, but be confident that you'll get the support you'll need—via your boss, books, or training. Don't reveal all your insecurities and weaknesses when the boss asks you. Don't say, "I'm not sure I can do this," or even, "I'll try." You will do well! You don't want him to know you're not a confident go-getter!

■ **"Will I be given what I need to be successful?"** Figure out what you will need to be successful and satisfied in the job. Maybe you want a few hours each week to continue writing code. Whatever it is, negotiate for what you need to do the job well—or don't take the promotion.

If the answer to any of these is "no," you can turn the promotion down without barring yourself from future opportunities. Explain how the company would benefit most by keeping you where you are right now. Point out the challenges or problems you still want to tackle, or the opportunities you want to explore. Position your "no" as what's best for the company, not what's best for you.

Ask the Experts

I was asked to be acting director until the position could be filled permanently. Should I say yes? What if I don't want that job?

Just being asked has propelled you into a dangerous situation. If you refuse, you can be seen as not committed to the organization. You almost have to say yes—but remember to negotiate for what you need to do a job you may not want (for example, time to do some of the current work you love, adequate resources and support, or the date when you will return to your original job). Another issue: Do you want the permanent director job? If no, say so when you are accepting the acting position. If you do, go ahead and apply, but recognize that if you don't get the job, you may be forced to leave the organization. Often there's no going back to your old position. Why? You may be seen as a potential threat to the new director or a potential disgruntled employee.

My boss has asked me to take over one line of the business that is in real financial trouble. I am worried that if I don't turn it around I will be fired. Is there any way I can get some promise of job security if I fail?

Probably not, but there are many things you can negotiate for. Require a 6-, 12-, and 18-month performance review of you and the business. That way, you're assured of getting face time with the boss so you can explain what you've been doing. Negotiate for the specific targets you're trying to hit. You also need to specify what "turnaround" means, since it could mean very different things to you and your boss, and his idea could be totally unreasonable. Does it mean reducing monthly losses by 5 percent or making a 20 percent profit? Finally, make sure to negotiate for what you'll need to be successful: the right to hire more people, purchase equipment, or demonstrate unilateral decision power. At least by specifying what you need, if the boss says "no," you've pointed out how he's limiting your ability to reach his goals.

now what do I do?

I love my company and the work I do, but it's a small organization and I have advanced as far as I can. What should I do?

This is a common problem for people who work in small organizations or ones with little turnover; people in such companies find there's no way to go up the ladder because their boss isn't leaving anytime soon or they're in the senior-most position for their type of work. For many folks, that's a clear signal that it's time to find new opportunities elsewhere.

If you want to stay, however, you could create a new career path for yourself: Write a new job description that includes new responsibilities that you are interested in doing, and give it a new title, then sell it to senior management. Or you can ask to be on new committees and projects. You can also take on more responsibility outside of work in professional organizations. The goal is to keep growing: It keeps you energized and builds your résumé for when you are ready to move.

Last year I became the vice president of my professional association. This two-year position is the normal route to the presidency. However, the demands made on the current president are so tremendous that I'm not sure I want the job. How can I figure out if the role is right for me?

You are smart to look ahead and to assess the situation realistically, since it is better to change your mind now rather than after you've been promoted. You might begin by talking with the current president and asking her about those tasks that take considerable time. Is there a current project, such as a strategic planning project, that is eating up her time and will be finished when you would take office? Can part of the job be delegated? Could staff be hired to take tasks off the president's shoulders? (The current president might like that suggestion!) If the president and other board members believe there is no way to relieve the burden on the president, then you will need to base your decision on your assessment of the current job, because it will likely be the same when you come on board.

I'm switching to a new department. My old department wants to give me a going-away party, but I really don't want one. Do I have to let them do it?

Yes, because the party isn't about you, it's about them. Sure, they want to show you that you'll be missed and that your contributions have been appreciated. But in reality "going-away" parties are designed to help the people left behind deal with their feelings of anxiety (what will your replacement be like to work with?), abandonment (particularly when the organization is doing poorly), and sadness (they will actually miss you). "Going-away" parties also signal to the rest of the organization that people are valued and treated with respect. So enjoy your party, and be prepared to give a brief speech thanking people for your experience. Be sure to mention how you plan to stay in touch.

Helpful Resources

WEB SITES

Radin Associates
www.radinassociates.com
A number of useful articles about career issues.

JobStar.org
www.jobstar.org
Contains the largest collection of salary surveys online.

Career Journal
www.careerjournal.com
Provides salary guides and articles on negotiation.

Salary.com
www.salary.com
Purchase personal salary reports here.

Bureau of Labor Statistics
www.bls.gov
The U.S. Department of Labor Web site provides useful salary information.

BOOKS

The Lessons of Experience: How Successful Executives Develop on the Job
by Morgan W. McCall Jr., Michael M. Lombardo, and Ann M. Morrison

The Empowered Manager: Positive Political Skills at Work
by Peter Block

The Shadow Negotiation: How Women Can Master the Hidden Agendas that Determine Bargaining Success
by Deborah Kolb, Ph.D., and Judith Williams, Ph.D.

Everyday Negotiation
by Deborah Kolb, Ph.D., and Judith Williams, Ph.D.

Nice Girls Don't Get the Corner Office: 101 Unconscious Mistakes Women Make that Sabotage Their Careers
by Lois P. Frankel

Moving on: new job, new company

Focus on your future 154
Are you headed in the right direction?

How healthy is my company? 156
Anticipating job upheaval

Looking ahead 158
Keep one eye on the horizon

When a recruiter calls 160
Know what they want

Analyze your future employer 162
Which company is right for you?

Reviving a stalled career 164
Learn to read the warning signs

Choosing to leave 166
When it's time to make a break

Changing careers 168
What if your next step is in a new direction?

Saying good-bye 170
Leave them with a good image of you

Smooth exits 172
Tying up loose ends

Now what do I do? 174
Answers to common questions

focus on your future

The responsibility to manage and optimize your career is clearly in your hands now, which means you have difficult questions to ask yourself—especially if you're thinking about or needing to make a career move.

These days, there's a good chance that your next career move won't be up into your boss's position. People no longer typically advance in a straight line through the ranks. More likely, you will make a lateral move into a new project team or a new department—or even more likely, you will move up by joining a new company.

That's why it's important that you assess how you are doing in your career so far. Asking yourself some questions will help guide you when you are considering making a move up in your own company or to another. Consider these four tough career-related questions:

■ **What are my strengths and talents?** Are you, for example, a skilled public speaker who enjoys persuading an audience to your way of thinking? Or is your talent in writing a critique of a speech?

■ **What do my past accomplishments tell me about my skills?** Think back to the top five successful projects you've completed in your career and try to recall the skills you used or developed to achieve your goals. What patterns have repeated themselves in your career? This should give you insight into your strongest skills.

■ **What do I value most in my career?** Is your main goal to earn large sums of money? Or would you rather make sufficient money while still being able to spend time with your family and friends?

■ **What is my vision of my work life?** Is it, for example, important for you to help others and to make the world a better place, not caring how much money you make? Or do you imagine starting and owning your own business, growing it to employ large numbers of people and making substantial sums of money?

Feedback from others

The next step is to ask people whom you trust to give you feedback on your strengths and weaknesses. There are two good ways to go about this:

Ask for feedback from a colleague Plan on spending a half hour with a colleague who is a good listener and who knows you well. First, talk about your accomplishments with him. There are two important aspects to this. The first is articulating your strengths and hearing yourself put into words what you have been thinking. And the second is to receive feedback. What would your colleague add to your skill list? Often people will see talents that you missed. This will help you refine your list of skills.

Ask colleagues to write letters about your accomplishments Again, turn to people whom you trust for this exercise, who will carefully consider what they say and how they express themselves. Ask these colleagues to answer the following questions about you:

- What are your strengths? Give examples.
- What attributes do they think might hold you back in your career?
- What career do they believe will bring you the most satisfaction?

Read the letters and see what patterns emerge. What language do they use to describe your strengths? Do others see your strengths as you do?

If others see your strengths as you do, consider this a confirmation of your talents. If they see your capabilities differently or consistently use different language to describe them, then you must decide if you agree with their assessments. Even if you don't, most likely you'll learn something valuable about how others view you.

In your career notebook ideas, write down your thoughts about this exercise and think about what the results say about your career.

how healthy is my company?

The signs of downsizing

Great! You've got your career in shape. Now what about the company you are currently working for? What kind of shape is it in? What are its strengths and weaknesses? Is your company well respected by its suppliers and loved by its customers? Does it have a healthy bottom line? Can it survive a market downturn? There are three steps to diagnosing the health of an organization.

1. Gather the facts from outside sources. Today it is easy to get newspaper stories, books, and Internet news about organizations, especially those that are publicly traded. It is your personal responsibility to know the facts about your organization.

2. Talk with customers, suppliers, and employees about the organization. Like people, organizations have reputations. Try asking people who have direct contact with an organization, such as customers and vendors, direct questions like, "How do you like doing business with our company?" If you know any employees of the company, talk to them, too. Listen carefully for both positive and negative feedback.

3. Know the financial health of the organization. You need to know if your company is financially sound. If it is a publicly traded for-profit organization, this information is easy to gather at Web sites such as **www.hoovers.com** or **www.vault.com**.

If you find that the diagnosis is not good, it may be time to move to a healthier organization.

When layoffs loom

It's one thing to know when you want to move on. It's another thing when your company is going to make that decision for you. Watch for the warning signs, because you can benefit by anticipating that you may be laid off.

How so? You gain time to prepare to negotiate a better **severance package** (a closing financial settlement between you and your employer). Lead time also allows you to land a new job before a pink slip lands on your desk.

So what should be on your radar screen? Rev up your job search if you notice these changes in the company's competition, finances, or structure:

■ The company's **profitability,** revenues, or market position has been declining for more than six months.

■ The company has experienced a **setback,** such as having a new drug rejected, not having a grant renewed, being sued, work stoppages, or major strikes.

■ The company has been **restructured**: New management has been brought in, layers of management eliminated, and the chain of command redrawn.

■ The company is involved in negotiations over **mergers**, **acquisitions**, or **takeovers**.

■ The company has received **bad press** because senior management has been indicted for illegal practices.

Often these situations are visible in the workplace in the form of:

■ Hiring freezes, in which vacated slots go unfilled

■ Spending freezes and budget cuts

■ Rise in security staff (who may eventually be called on to escort laid-off employees off the premises)

■ Closed door or off-site meetings of senior management

■ Important projects being put on hold

■ Products being pulled off the shelves

looking ahead

Manage your current job—and the next one

Because moving out of your current job at your present company is often the only way to get the right career experience, you need to take time every now and then to research where you want to go next and prepare yourself for that next step. Even if you don't foresee an imminent leap to a new job, it's a good idea to routinely scan the following media to keep yourself on your toes:

The general news media When you listen to or read the news, ask yourself these questions: What does this tell me about jobs? What companies and industries are expanding? What part of the country is growing? What legislation is coming down the pike, and how will it impact companies and the job market?

Newspaper want ads Even though only 20 percent of job openings are advertised in newspapers, you can still learn a lot about the job marketplace. What new types of jobs are being created? What's happening to salaries? What companies are hiring? Periodically pick up a large newspaper from another part of the country and compare their job listings to your local ones.

Company Web sites Make a list of 20 companies that you'd like to work for and regularly scan their Web sites for news, developments, and opportunities.

Employment Web sites Routinely scan job sites like **monster.com, careerjournal.com, hotjobs.com,** or **mbajungle.com.** If your boss already knows you're looking for a job, post your résumé on these sites to test how marketable you are.

Specialty want ads Subscribe to professional or trade journals and read their employment ads so you can see what's available in your field.

Become a trend-watcher

Gather information on economic, global, and financial trends by subscribing to the following Web sites. Most offer a free trial:

www.WallStreetJournal.com

www.shapingtomorrow.com

www.bizintelligencepipe line.com

www.trendwatching.com

www.forecasts.org

Keep your résumé up to date

Don't wait until you've got an interview lined up to dust off your **résumé**! Collect examples and craft stories about your accomplishments, then update your résumé quarterly so you'll be ready to grab any opportunity that comes your way. Powerful résumés include these components:

Profile statement In two or three sentences, describe what you will offer your next employer. This profile is often the only part that gets read during the winnowing-down process. Avoid vagueness; use the attention-grabbing buzz-words that a future employer or a résumé search program will pick up. Also include your key skills and strengths, a summary of your work experience, and a description of what you bring to the workplace. Include foreign languages spoken and accreditations.

> **Example**
>
> Mission-driven development professional with expertise in higher education. Proven ability to cultivate and build relationships with high-net-worth alumni. More than 10 years of experience managing fund-raising campaigns with strict deadlines and ambitious goals. Past accomplishments due to:
>
> - Superior writing skills
> - MBA in finance
> - Fluency in Spanish and French
> - Knowledge of database technology

Experience A list of job duties is boring, but a list of what you accomplished by performing those duties is powerful! Translate what you did into a summary of what you contributed to the company, again using key words. Ask, "How was the project, client, company, and bottom line better off as a result of my action?"

> **Example:**
>
> Instead of writing about your job function:
>
> - "Served on a cross-functional team for marketing and sales"
>
> make it more powerful by writing:
>
> - "By bridging the gap between marketing and sales via a cross-functional team, reduced the average time-to-market of new products by three months"

when a recruiter calls

Know what a recruiter is looking for

There will come a time in your career when you get a phone call from an executive recruiter. That's a good thing. It means you are reaching the level of high visibility in your industry. It means your name is becoming known in your field.

Because headhunters and recruiters usually only contact employed people, chances are they will call you at work. Getting a call at work about other jobs can be disconcerting and make you anxious. But don't panic: Consider it an opportunity to network; that's how

recruiters look at it. (In fact, headhunters may not be calling to recruit you, but rather to ask you for names of colleagues who might be candidates for a job in your field that would not suit you. Should that happen, think twice before you give out the names of your fellow colleagues or friends. You might want to check with them first.)

If a headhunter calls you at work, listen politely, but resist the urge to talk openly with her about any job possibilities or name referrals. Instead, give her your home number and arrange another time to talk. Ask her to e-mail the job specifics to your personal account.

When you talk again in a private setting, realize the headhunter may know very little about your actual background or current position. Explain what she needs to know and then ask for specifics about the job, such as salary range, and whether relocation is involved. Recruiters usually specialize in certain industries (such as advertising or retail) or certain types of jobs (e.g., only accountants or computer programmers). Because of their specialization, they can be great sources of information about what is going on in your particular industry or profession. This is a great time to pick her brain about where the good jobs are going. If you do decide to go forward with this recruiter, ask about what stage the search is at and what the next steps are.

Ask the Experts

I was really interested in this one job, but I can't relocate now. I am worried that if I turn this great opportunity down, this recruiter won't ever call me again. How do I handle this?

If you are not interested in the job, explain why. The recruiter will not be upset, especially if you say there may come a time when you can relocate. You are inventory to them; the more they have, the better. Chances are he will check in with you from time to time, to see how you are doing or for referrals. You can do the same.

What is the difference between an executive search firm and a recruiting firm?

Executive search firms (also called placement firms) specialize in finding people to fill vacancies at the boardroom level. They recruit VPs, CEOs, and directors. Recruiters typically are used to fill supervisory and middle management positions.

Who pays the recruiting firm if I decide to take the job?

The company that hired the firm to fill the vacancy pays.

FIRST PERSON SUCCESS STORY

Moving on with the same boss

I've had the same boss at four different companies and across two different business sectors. Alex first hired me for sales at a small telecommunications company. After three years he was called by an executive headhunter to see if he wanted to be CEO of a start-up healthcare company. He did, and he hired me to lead new-market development. After four years we both moved into pharmaceuticals; he brought 10 of his former employees, and I brought four of my own people, creating my own loyalty group. By getting the attention of a strong leader and continually proving loyalty and competence, I've become a critical part of his team—wherever he goes.

—Steve C., New York, NY

analyze your future employer

Make sure you look before you leap

Okay, you are ready to move on. You found a great opportunity or perhaps a recruiter found it for you. Either way, you are really keen to take this new job. However, before you get too far along, take some time to investigate this potential new employer. How do they operate? What type of corporate culture (see pages 34–35) do they have?

To answer these questions, check out their Web site, annual reports, and marketing materials. What do they say about the company's values? Do they talk about bottom line, or refer to the company as a "family"? Are the materials themselves bold and colorful? This says they are very image conscious. Are they simple and not very frivolous? That may indicate a company where innovation and speed-to-market are valued. If there are photos, do the people look conservative and subdued? This may indicate a slower-moving, change-resistant organization.

Use your network (see pages 124–129) to see if you can find anyone in the company and then contact her for information. When you call or e-mail the employee, mention your mutual contact and ask a few nonthreatening, open-ended questions about the workplace. The surest way to get the truth about what it's like to work for a company is to talk to the employees.

Look for other clues. Everything in a company's environment is a clue to what is important there. When you go for your interviews, start by examining the parking lot: Are there reserved spaces for the president and VPs? If so, hierarchy may be important. Do employees labor silently in cubicles, or do they chat casually across an open-plan layout? This may tell you something about the amount and type of interaction that is valued there.

Where to find out more

To get more information about an organization's history, financial health, and future plans, check the following places:

Web sites:

SEC filings and forms (EDGAR) (**www.sec.gov/edgar.shtml**). This links to companies' public filings, and provides instructions for searching its database.

AnnualReports.com (**www.reportgallery.com/**). This site allows individual and institutional investors to access online annual reports for free.

CNN/Money—**http://money.cnn.com/**

Yahoo! Finance—**http://finance.yahoo.com/**

BigCharts—**http://bigcharts.marketwatch.com/**

Library databases:

Bloomberg This powerful online database, accessed through a stand-alone terminal in your library, provides minute-by-minute financial news and in-depth financial information on over 150,000 public companies worldwide, as well as on indexes, bonds, governments, and much more.

Lexis-Nexis This fee-based subscription database allows users to do full-text searches of international, national, and regional newspapers, wire services, broadcast transcripts; U.S. federal and state cases, laws, codes, regulations; legal news reviews; Shepard's Citations® for all U.S. Supreme Court cases back to 1789; SEC filings and reports; medical news; and non-English-language news and legal sources.

Mergent Online This database is a suite of information resources that enables in-depth business and financial research on U.S.-based and non-U.S. companies.

Wall Street Journal (Available in the ABI-Inform Global database) The financial newspaper of record, the WSJ offers in-depth coverage of national and international finance and hard news.

Industry surveys from Standard & Poor's Net Advantage These surveys of leading companies in each industry contain tables listing historical financial data, including revenues and income, profitability ratios, and balance sheet ratios.

reviving a stalled career

Staying alert on
your career path

You're cruising down the career path of your dreams when—bam!—you hit a major obstacle in the road. You get a new boss or you get moved to a new department. There's talk of the company downsizing. Whatever it is, it brings you to a dead halt. If only you'd been watching the road, you'd have seen the danger sign a mile back and taken a different route. But you didn't. Now what?

One critical component to managing your career is being able to see those red flags and act on them before they hurt you. The two common career problems below are often preceded by warning signs. These signs should be a clear indication that trouble may be on the horizon:

Your career may be at a standstill . . . if you're bored with your work, in a "dead-end" job, work for a miserable boss, work at an exhausting pace, or work in a demoralizing environment.

Your job may be on the line . . . if there are rumors of mergers and acquisitions, downsizing, layoffs, outsourcing, or bankruptcies.

By looking for and recognizing the red flags, you can keep your career moving forward and minimize the bumps along the way. But in order to do this, you need to understand why you might ignore those red flags in the first place.

Career traps

There are two kinds of traps that may be preventing you from reading career red flags or acting on them:

Trade-offs Sometimes trade-offs are necessary; for example, you may decide to stay in a low-paying job because it has **flextime** that allows you take care of your children. The point is to know when the trade-offs are not worth it. If you find yourself stuck in a stifling job, always ask yourself whether it's worth it to stay in this job because . . .

- You enjoy the close commute

- You have a huge debt to pay off

- You need the benefits (insurance, tuition reimbursement)

- Your stock options and pension are nearly vested

- The economy is bad or the job market is slow

- The job offers you security as a single parent or provider

- You need to focus your real energies elsewhere

Attitude Your decision to stay in a job may also be influenced by attitudes or beliefs that prevent you from reading your current situation accurately. Again, ask yourself if you are staying in this job because you think . . .

- It isn't any better anywhere else (cynicism)

- It's better to stay with "the devil you know" (resignation)

- It can't be bad forever; it's always "darkest before the dawn" (unrealistic optimism)

- It's not that bad; it can't get any worse (denial)

- I won't be able to do well in a new job at a new company (fear)

- I can't dump all my work on my colleagues (overinvestment)

- I would be giving up and admitting defeat (pride)

- It's out of my hands; "what will be will be" (abdication)

Rarely will acting on these attitudes produce the best decision for your career.

choosing to leave

Knowing when it's time to move on

How do you know when it's time to get out of a job or a company? If any of these describe your current situation, you'd probably be happier elsewhere:

- You and your boss have a "rocky" relationship and no amount of effort has improved your ability to work better together.

- You have an ongoing conflict with a colleague with no likely resolution in sight.

- You have been passed over for a promotion, bonus, or raise that you were promised or have clearly earned. When you asked why, you received a questionable or unacceptable explanation.

- A new layer of management has been added, and you now report to a new person between you and your old boss.

- You've "capped out" your career opportunities in the company, or your only opportunity for advancement is into your boss's job, and he's not retiring anytime soon.

- You don't get any recognition for your good work, or worse, your boss takes credit for your work.

- You no longer get plum assignments or high-visibility projects, or are asked to attend critical meetings.

- Access to management is getting harder and harder. Your e-mails and phone calls aren't returned, and that "open door" policy isn't open for you.

- Office politics is overwhelming and you feel that you can't trust anyone because you've been backstabbed repeatedly by colleagues.

- You haven't learned anything new in the last six months.

- You suspect that the company is heading toward a severe economic downturn.

Ask the Experts

I've been feeling sidelined and phased out at work ever since our company "reorganized." Are there any signs I should look for that might tell me my job is not secure?

Every company goes through a period of reorganization or "right-sizing"—or any of the other euphemisms for layoffs. Here are some common warning signs that could mean you might be the next one to go:

- Have you had perks or privileges taken away?
- Do you no longer get invited to meetings as in the past?
- Are decisions made without your input, or worse, with the input of your peers or direct reports?
- Has your office been moved to the remote recesses of the company footprint?
- Are you spending more time working alone?
- Have key parts of your job been allocated to others? Was it even positioned as "freeing you up for bigger tasks in the future"?
- Have you recently received a performance appraisal that was substantially lower than in the past?
- Has the boss's secretary or assistant stopped joking or being friendly with you?

Sometimes there's a silver lining

Bad news for your organization can translate into bad news for your job, but not necessarily. Often these upheavals represent great career opportunities. For example, one large telecommunications company seeking to reduce its workforce offered a **management buyout**. Over four times the number of employees they expected chose to leave. This left huge opportunities for ambitious employees who wanted to stay. They were then promoted into vacated positions. However, a word to the wise: It's often prudent to take the offer and go, because management buyouts usually signal organizational distress. If enough people don't take the offer, layoffs often follow. And the buyout offer will usually be more attractive than what's offered to those who are laid off.

changing careers

The bigger the leap, the bigger the effort

You've been steadily working away at your career for a while now and you are starting to feel dissatisfied with it. (You are not alone—people change careers three to seven times in their lifetime.) Perhaps it is the industry you chose to work in that is causing the problems. Maybe you are tired of all the changes in healthcare or finance or retailing. Or perhaps you love your industry, but you are growing tired of specializing in a particular area of work, such as accounting or sales or research. Some people go further and change both their jobs and their choice of industry.

But rather than changing both the function of your job (sales, HR, finance) and your industry (healthcare, education, technology), experts advise that you change one, build experience, and then change the other. That way you're asking your future employer to make a shorter leap of faith in hiring you.

How do you convince a future employer to hire you when you don't have the past performance (in that job or industry) to predict future success?

Take incremental steps and build some related experience Start doing things now to build some exposure to the new field: Join a professional organization related to your next industry (great for networking, too!). Take on projects at your current job that expose you to a new functional area. Offer to work as an intern—you get to build your skills, while the company gets to check you out. Volunteer at a nonprofit organization to learn administrative or management skills you're lacking.

Identify transferable skills Many skills you've learned in one industry can be reapplied in another.

Build your knowledge Learn everything you can about your desired job or industry. Subscribe to the appropriate professional and trade magazines and regularly check relevant Web sites. Consider taking courses toward the appropriate academic degree or certification.

Interviewing: The basic questions you need to answer

Remember that interviews are actually two-way conversations in which a potential employer is deciding whether to hire you and you are deciding whether you want to work there.

Bottom line, the employer is trying to determine:

- Do you have the skills to perform the job?

- Are you motivated to do the work?

- Would we like working with you and would you fit into our organization?

These questions are especially important if you are trying to change careers. You need to prove that the experience you have in one career will transfer to another. To do that, relate five of your best success stories that show how your skills and achievements will work in this new career. Choose stories where you've shown initiative, tackled new challenges, learned quickly, and shown resourcefulness in the face of uncertainty. These are all skills that will serve you well in a new job. Then explicitly point out what you can do for them based on past successes. Say, "For you, this means . . . " and segue into how they will similarly benefit. For more on success stories, see page 141.

At the same time, you need to determine:

- Do I have the skill set needed for this job, and if not, will I be able to develop it?

- Will I look forward to going to work each morning?

- Will I like working with these people and for this organization?

Every organization has different interview procedures, so ask HR early on about what to expect. In the first round, you may meet first with the HR manager. In the second round you may meet with your future boss, peers, and subordinates. You might then go on to round three: meeting the boss's boss.

Every time you interview, you'll need to answer their three fundamental questions and get answers to yours. Prepare ahead of time: Peruse books with typical interview questions, craft answers, and practice them out loud.

saying good-bye

Never burn bridges as you leave

You've landed your next great job. Good for you! Now it's time to tell your current employer that you're leaving. Most likely this will involve at least two conversations: one with your boss and one with Human Resources. Before you say good-bye, check out how your company handles resignations.

Your goal in both conversations is to not burn bridges, but to leave with solid relationships intact. Why? Because someday you may find yourself returning to the company, or your boss may be the hiring manager at another company you interview with in the future, or you may need a recommendation. Be gracious and courteous. First, set a meeting with your boss. Behind closed doors, tell her that you are taking another job when you leave.

Say good-bye to your boss privately
Offer to do whatever is necessary to make the transition go smoothly. Thank her for her support. This is not the time to bring up any complaints about her as a boss, your coworkers, or the organization. In some companies, this kind of conversation triggers immediate action, such as a meeting with HR. Some companies also have policies in place that require departing employees to clean out their offices the same day they announce their resignation to ensure that the resigning employee doesn't leave with any confidential information.

Prepare for an unceremonious evacuation Everyone's heard stories about employees being escorted out of the building by security guards 10 minutes after handing in their resignations. On the off chance this could happen to you, take home personal items, files, and examples of your work beforehand. This includes electronic files: E-mail them to your new address, or upload them and store them online until you can download them. Visit **www.yahoo.com** and other Internet services for more info on online storage.

Counteroffers

If you have a skill critical to the organization, there's a good chance that you may be given a **counteroffer**, but don't be flattered. In most cases it's not about what's best for you (why did they wait till the last minute to make things better for you?), it's about what's best for the company.

There are many reasons not to accept a counteroffer. First of all, most people don't leave their jobs because of money. It's usually dissatisfaction with the boss, the work, or the organization. Those things won't change with a salary increase. Accepting a counteroffer can also have a negative career impact: Inside the company, your loyalty may forever be questioned and you may lose your place in the inner circle. Externally, your reputation (with the jilted company, or the recruiter who was trying to place you) will also be tarnished.

Try to avoid being offered a counteroffer in the first place. How do you do this? Tell management far in advance if you're unhappy in your job so they have time to improve the situation and won't feel blackmailed into making a counteroffer when you resign.

No matter what, however, you have the right to make your own decision about a counteroffer. Know the costs and benefits of staying. If you've generally been satisfied in your old job and have a very specific thing you'd like changed, go ahead and negotiate. Come in with very clear requirements and stick to your guns. Don't allow yourself to be guilt-tripped or coerced out of what you feel is best for you.

Letters of resignation

While not required, writing **letters of resignation** has become common practice. This letter can be as simple as, "Effective on [date], I am resigning. . ." No explanation is necessary. If you do want to explain your departure, use positive and nonaccusatory language, such as, "I'm looking for a new challenge." Many organizations use the date on this letter to determine outstanding vacation and benefits and to trigger the replacement hiring process. You can read from this letter if you are worried about your boss's reaction. Spend some time on it, since it goes in your permanent personnel file and cements your reputation at your old company.

smooth exits

Cleaning house before you leave

How you leave a job can impact your career just as much as how you start one. Here's how to leave the door open and your reputation intact when you move on:

Transition your work Finish outstanding projects or note the status of ongoing accounts or projects. If you have accumulated specialized knowledge, write it up or share it verbally. Offer to train your successor if there's a crossover period; this shows the company one last time what a great contributor you were. And if you're still job searching, mention your wrap-up work to future employers as an example of your professionalism.

Distance yourself Negotiate with your boss about how to slowly reduce your job duties. Be prepared to delete passwords and access codes to file servers and high-security areas to distance yourself from sensitive documents. This protects you from being blamed for any mistakes made during your final two weeks or from accusations that you took or misused information.

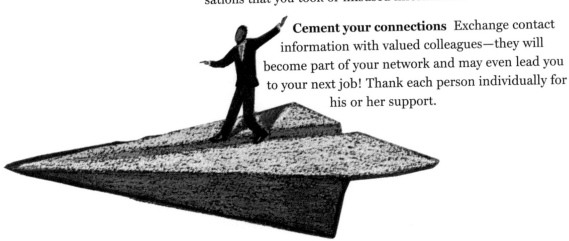

Cement your connections Exchange contact information with valued colleagues—they will become part of your network and may even lead you to your next job! Thank each person individually for his or her support.

Ask the Experts

I've deleted all my personal files, such as my résumé, off my company computer before leaving. Am I covered?

Most definitely not! If you are leaving behind the company PC, consider purchasing software like Cyberscrub to erase everything from your hard drive. You should also click on "clear history" in your browser. Deleting e-mail and dragging sensitive material into the trash does not destroy files. After you're gone, your old employer can still see which Web sites you've visited and read every file or e-mail you've written, received, downloaded, or forwarded unless you take the actions described above.

Exit interviews

As your time draws to a close, HR may request an **exit interview** with you in which they will ask you to discuss your employment experiences and reasons for leaving. As with any interview, you need to approach this with some finesse. Here are some guidelines:

Be positive An exit interview is not the time to purge all the unhappiness or bitterness you feel about the company. Even if you're leaving because of a terrible boss or low pay, be careful what you say. Many career counselors advise keeping complaints to yourself, since spilling them can do you no good at this point, and may even come back to haunt you when you need a reference from your old boss later on.

Be constructive If you really do need to get some things off your chest, then talk proactively and strategically, instead of griping about how terribly you've been treated. Turn your complaints into positive suggestions for changes.

Be mindful Your goal is to leave the company gracefully with solid relationships intact. You never know where former coworkers may end up; that HR director conducting your exit interview today may be the same one who interviews you at another company five years from now!

now what do I do?

I don't want my boss to know I'm looking for a job, but at some point I will need him as a reference? What can I do?

There are several ways to handle this common problem. One way, if asked by a potential employer, is to be up front and state, "I'd like to hold off on using my boss as a reference until you foresee extending me a job offer." In the meantime, you can use other people as references, such as vendors, clients, colleagues, and previous bosses. Copies of performance appraisals written by your current boss can also be helpful.

What if an interviewer asks why I'm leaving my current profession?
You're right to be prepared now for this question. Some guidelines:

- If you are pursuing a lifelong dream, say, "I've always wanted to work in this field, and I've been preparing for the change for the last five years. Some things I've done include . . . "

- If you are trying to escape a struggling industry, say, "I've enjoyed working in that industry, but it's clear that opportunities for growth and challenge are getting scarce, and constant learning and growing are important for me."

I just gave notice that I'll be leaving for a new job in two weeks, but I still have four weeks of vacation left. Do I have to forfeit all that?

No. Just because you are the one who decided to leave does not mean the company doesn't have to give you what you're owed. First, review your own records and clearly define how many vacation, personal, or sick days you have earned but not used. Second, set up a meeting with HR to determine the number of days you are owed and ask if that can be converted into salary.

I was thrilled to be offered a job as an account manager—until I heard the salary offer! It's 30 percent less than what I'm making as a budget analyst. What's the deal?

Your current salary reflects the industry experience and skills you've built up over time, so as a new account manager, you'll have to climb the salary ladder again as you build expertise. And you may have to be willing to take the cut to get into a new career. But this doesn't mean you can't negotiate now for future salary growth. Get a commitment for a performance review in three to six months, and identify what you would need to be producing by then to merit what kind of salary increase.

My company is offering a financial deal for people to voluntarily leave. Should I take it?

There are lots of reasons you may want to take the offer: having the time off to recharge, go on an adventure, spend time with family, or to do a full-time job search. When considering the offer, identify clearly what you will do with your newfound time. Next, look over your expenses to see if the offer will allow you to do what you want to do. Finally, recognize that it generally takes on average one month of serious job searching for every $10,000 of salary you want in your next job. So if you do plan to go back to work, keep that in mind when determining how long the offer allows you to play before beginning a job search.

Helpful Resources

WEB SITES

I-resign.com
www.i-resign.com
Templates for all kinds of resignation letters and job search letters, calculators for determining what the company owes you financially, plus a mother lode of advice for making an electronic transition, such as eliminating all traces of your Internet activity on the company PC.

Radin Associates
www.radinassociates.com
Features a number of useful articles about career issues.

The Riley Guide
www.rileyguide.com
This provides many links to Web sites that help you with relocation issues like computing the cost of living, finding schools, comparing real estate, and getting relocation packages.

Brain Reserve
www.faithpopcorn.com
The thought-provoking site of futurist Faith Popcorn, this site covers technology advancement, new products, and new developments in society.

America's Career InfoNet
www.acinet.org/acinet/oview1.asp
Forecasts for the fastest-growing jobs in the U.S.

BOOKS

Barnes & Noble Basics: Résumés and Cover Letters
by Susan Stellin

Barnes & Noble Basics: Your Job Interview
by Cynthia Ingols and Mary Shapiro

Career Bounce Back!
by J. Damian Birkel with Stacy Miller

Firing Back
by Jodie-Beth Galos and Sandy McIntosh, Ph.D.

How to Shine at Work
by Linda Dominguez

CHAPTER 9

Finding your balance

The right mix for you 178
Knowing what you want

Balancing work and life 180
Are you trying to do too much?

Alternative career paths 182
You are still a committed worker

Short-term challenges 184
When your family needs you

Making big changes 186
When the change is long term

Telecommuting 188
Negotiating the when and where of work

Taking early retirement 190
It requires a lot of forethought

Now what do I do? 192
Answers to common questions

the right mix for you

Know what's important to you

People with careers are working to achieve certain goals. Being a part of a work community may be the most compelling reason for you to go to work in the morning. Or maybe money is the key. Whatever your values are, they may last your entire working life, or they may shift as your circumstances change.

What makes your day-to-day work meaningful? Looking at your work history and asking, "Why did I work at this job?" will tease your motivators for working. You may work to:

- receive **recognition** for a job well done
- enjoy the **work itself**
- feel needed by **having responsibility**
- create **order and structure** to your day
- get the **status** the job title, profession, or employer conveys
- take on the **challenge** of overcoming obstacles and problems
- use your **creativity** and innovation
- have **power and influence** in making decisions
- be stimulated and grow **intellectually**
- have a **variety** of activities to keep life interesting
- achieve **respect and self-worth** in a culture that values work
- feel a sense of **accomplishment** when achieving a goal
- relieve boredom
- **grow** your skills and expertise
- be part of a **community** with meaningful relationships
- make a **positive impact** in your community or in people's lives
- create **security** against an uncertain future

Your evolving values

Whatever your values are, they will change over the course of your lifetime. If you are like many people, your values may shift in the following ways:

- Your first apartment, your first car—both required a paycheck. Money was your primary motivator.

- As you achieved some financial stability, you may have started to wrestle with some basic career decisions: "What do I really want to do? Where do I want to live?" You may have been in a job you hated and learned not only what you didn't want in a job, but also what you needed. A workaholic cutthroat work environment may have revealed your desire for positive work relationships. A boss that took credit for all your work may have revealed your need for recognition.

- The rewards you were looking for in a job became more defined and you may have begun to choose jobs that would give you what you wanted. The need for achievement drove you to take a job with a start-up. The need for order and structure influenced you to become a certified public accountant. Work commitments were primary in your life so you looked for jobs that provided greater challenges.

- Along the way, you may have gotten married, had children, or developed an avocation for high-altitude climbing. That 60-hour-a-week job suddenly didn't give you the time for these outside passions. You may have shifted to a job with more flexibility or negotiated a part-time position.

- As your finances became secure, you may have decided to find an opportunity (paid or unpaid) to give back to the community. Or as you grew bored of having the same career for 20 years, you sought out work that would provide new stimulation.

balancing work and life

What's right for you?

Balancing your work and your family life can be a huge challenge. The demands of both can be extremely pressing. How do you handle it? Remember that you alone should determine what's the right "balance" for you. Additionally, the word "balance" does not demand equality. At any one point in your life, you may be more focused on your work, happily putting in 60-hour workweeks and traveling Monday through Friday. At another point you may be primarily taking care of an aging mother and doing contract work on the side. What's critical is knowing yourself.

It's also important for you to know how you view these two aspects of your life. Some people are inclined to be "**career integrators**," while others are "**career separators**." Integrators are people who do not make clear distinctions between their work and their family life, while separators make clear demarcations.

There are two simple tests to determine your inclination. Look at your key holder. Do you have two key rings, one for work and another for home? If yes, then you a separator. If you have one ring that has work and home keys, then you are an integrator. Also, do you keep one or two calendars? If you have two, then you likely keep track of personal events in one calendar and work-related events in the other. Having two calendars is another sign of a separator.

Neither approach is right or wrong. But because integrators squish things together, they may not recognize that one area of their lives is being shortchanged. Separators, on the other hand, may expend unnecessary energy keeping their lives compartmentalized.

Changing the balance

Have you ever woken up and thought, "Wow! My life is out of control! Instead of working 60 hours per week, I want to work and enjoy softball games with my children." If you want to shift the balance in your life, think through and write down your responses to the following questions as a first step to change.

- **Which of my behaviors will I stop, start, or change?** Consider the behavior that you would like to change. If, for example, you want to put more focus on your personal life, then you may need to say "no" to more overtime. But saying "no" is not enough. Also make a positive commitment to your personal life by doing things like making plans for a day trip with friends.

- **What, specifically, am I willing to do?** Behaviors need to be clear and quantifiable. If you want to spend less time at work and more time with family and friends, set clear and measurable goals, such as: "My goal is to work 45 hours each week and spend five hours with friends." Then hold yourself accountable.

- **How will others support me?** Sharing your goals with other people will enable them to support you in making those changes, and will make your goals more concrete. When family and friends know about your goals, it gets a little harder for you to cheat!

- **How might I sabotage myself?** This is a very important question to answer honestly. Imagine that your goal is to go the gym three times per week. Now answer honestly why you might not make that happen. Realizing that you may unconsciously forget your gym clothes or accept invitations to happy hour with colleagues shows self-awareness about how you might undermine your own goals.

- **How will I reward myself when I reach my goal?** It is important to acknowledge your success in specific and satisfying ways.

alternative career paths

A new way of looking at your career

There may come a time when you know the healthiest choice for your life and your career is to create an alternative career path that will give you greater flexibility. There are many reasons for this: You may be facing a short-term personal crisis or a more long-term challenge. Either way, you do not intend to stop being a valued contributor; you just want to do your job in an alternative way, for example, by telecommuting.

When proposing an alternative career path in your organization (such as declining a promotion or seeking a lateral move), explain how your choice benefits the organization. This prevents you from being seen as "not ambitious" and being sidelined. Name the challenges you want to tackle or the opportunities you want to exploit. Leave the door open for future promotions by giving a time frame or a condition for when you would be ready to move up.

Next, negotiate for what you need. If it's time away from work you need, say "Yes, if I can continue to work four days a week." If it's hands-on research you want, negotiate for time in the lab.

FIRST PERSON SUCCESS STORY

Making work work for me

I had two small children at home and was feeling like I just could not continue on in my stressful, high-visibility role as VP of marketing. But when I first raised the possibility of flextime with my boss, he countered with, "We all work too much here—it's normal!" But I didn't think it was. So I set about convincing him how some norms in our fast-paced workplace were outdated. First, I subtly challenged the images of top performers who worked 80-hour weeks by putting the focus on how my way of working by project—rather than by hours—promoted innovation, reduced redundancies and errors, and stimulated initiative in others. I also questioned practices that supported outdated definitions of commitment—asking why staff meetings were held at 4:30 on Fridays—and offered more productive alternatives. For example, I suggested moving deadlines forward to avoid all-nighters and circulated articles about the hidden costs of work fatigue. My boss eventually got it and let me go to a four-day workweek!

—Melissa K., Kansas City, MO

Two-career choices

If you or your spouse or partner gets a job offer that requires relocating, ask these questions:

■ **Is one job portable?** Just as technological advances are moving jobs to India and China, these same technologies give some people flexibility in where they work. For example, if your spouse performs computer-related work, then it is possible that she can relocate and continue with her present job.

■ **Whose career will be primary?** If your career commands the larger reward in the marketplace, or if you have greater career ambitions than your spouse, you may choose to take the job offer, move the family, and your spouse can find a job when you both get there. Since dual-career couples are common today, it is likely that your new employer will volunteer to support your spouse's job hunt, or you can negotiate for that.

■ **Can you have jobs in different cities and a long-distance relationship?** This means that you will have two homes, two sets of friends, two mortgage payments, and many plane rides. A few people make this work; for most it is a short-term interim solution of a year or so.

If you and your spouse or partner are facing the decision, "Who is going to stay home with the children?" ask these questions:

■ **Whose career will be primary?** The answer to this should be influenced by whose career is ascending and whose may be waning, by whose income is more secure, and by whose income will best cover the lack of a second income. One of you may be thinking of taking time out to recharge your batteries or reflect on what career you want to pursue next.

■ **Who is better suited for at-home life?** If you love the high speed, high pressure of corporate life, staying at home may not fit your driving personality. Who has more affiliation needs that could be met at home instead of work? Who has the greater patience and energy to deal with young children?

■ **How will you reenter the workforce?** If you totally disengage from your professional life, reentry wll involve more effort. So think about how you can stay current by reading professional magazines, extending your education, maintaining an active role in a professional organization, or contracting out your services on a limited basis.

short-term challenges

When a crisis interrupts your working life

Your career is booming; your skills are top-notch and you know how to handle just about any job disaster your boss or the market can throw you. But what if the problem you are suddenly facing has to do with a family member, say, your teenage son who is having a problem with drugs or your elderly mother who has just broken her hip? Or what if you are having a health crisis, such as a case of pneumonia or a slipped disk? While the coping skills you learned on the job will help you weather these storms, you will most likely need outside help. Even if you don't talk about your troubles at work, it is inevitable that people will notice a change in your energy level, ability to concentrate, and general mood. Since you don't want to be labeled "unproductive" or "uncommitted" as you endure distress, consider taking these steps to protect yourself and find support at work:

Talk to your boss Since you may need to redefine your workload for the short term or take some weeks off, speak to your boss about your situation, the sooner the better. If people in your office have been cross-trained to perform your job responsibilities, ask about shifting your workload temporarily. Then get the support of your colleagues. Just as your boss should know about your situation, colleagues within your immediate work circle should also be informed. Decide with your boss how colleagues should be informed of your situation.

Contact your HR department If you need to take time off, an HR professional will be able to fill you in on the provisions of the **Family and Medical Leave Act** (FMLA). Although this bill was passed in the 1980s primarily to support new parents, caring for an aging parent is also allowable under the bill, along with caring for an ill spouse or child.

A family crisis can cause a great deal of emotional stress. If you or your family needs therapy, contact your company's referral services, or the Employee Assistance Program (EAP) for referrals. You can also access the Online Employee Assistance Directory at **www.eap-sap.com/eap**.

Finding help

If your work is suffering because you are finding yourself unable to cope with family pressures, or caring for ill family members, or if you are concerned about how having a baby will impact your job, know that there are resources out there:

The Family and Medical Leave Act The Family and Medical Leave Act (FMLA) requires that businesses with 50 or more people give new mothers 12 weeks of unpaid, job-guaranteed leave.

- **Paid maternity leave** is offered by the most progressive companies. Some companies even have short-term paid paternity leave.

- **Income protection programs** are a benefit offered by some companies that covers some or all income lost during maternity leave.

Eldercare Many baby-boomer employees are finding themselves caring for their aging parents, so organizations are beginning to support employees in different ways:

- **Referral services** assist employees in locating nursing homes, rehabilitation facilities, and home healthcare support systems.

- **Long-term care insurance** is a new benefit that organizations are offering in which employees can buy policies at group rates to protect their financial assets in retirement.

making big changes

Building a flexible workweek

For some people, a short-term crisis becomes a way of life that must be folded into the work/life balance, and this often means creating an alternative career path. You may have a spouse who has a chronic illness and needs your constant care. Or you may develop significant outside interests, like running marathons or spending some time each month being a house-parent at a teen halfway house. Regardless, the bottom line is the same: Your old work schedule is no longer desirable or possible. But you are still committed to your job. How do you work it out?

For these reasons, some organizations have created a variety of **flexible work arrangements**: policies and practices that allow employees to mold their workdays to the needs of their lives.

Flextime means organizing employees' starting and ending times around core business hours from, for example, 10 a.m. to 3 p.m. Employees can start at 7 a.m. and leave at 3 p.m., or start and leave later.

Compressed workweeks allow employees to work 40 hours in less than five days. This often means three days of 12-hour shifts and four days off.

Job-sharing programs are when two people share a single full-time position. The critical factor in the success of these programs is communication between the employees.

Part-time work involves committing to less than a 40-hour week. The critical question is whether the organization provides benefits, such as health insurance, to part-time employees.

Telecommuting is the option of working off-site, often in your home office. The requirements are a good technical interface (e-mail, phone, computer), excellent communication with the home office, and the ability to self-discipline to get the work done.

Help with child care

Many working parents choose to take time off from their careers because they want to raise their children; others are forced out because they can't find any viable child care. To keep working parents on board, many corporations have launched employee programs to help solve the ever growing need for quality child care. Here is a sample of what is available in many Fortune 500 companies:

■ **Referral services** assist employees in finding child-care centers, after-school programs, summer camps, emergency back-up care, and sick-child care.

■ **Subsidizing child care** is often offered on a sliding scale, with a company paying a larger proportion for employees with lower salaries.

■ **Contributing pretax dollars** to cover dependent-care expenses. This allows you to pay your child care provider with pretax dollars. It is another way that organizations can reduce the financial burdens of family life.

■ **On-site day care** allows parents to bring their kids to a day care facility that is located at their work. This allows parents the opportunity to see their children on their lunch hour, or arrange for additional supervision if a parent has to work late.

■ **Tween support** Organizations are recognizing that the "bigger the kids, the bigger the challenges" and are responding with new ways to support parents of preteens.

telecommuting

Owning your schedule

Thanks to technology, telecommuting is proving a great solution to those workers who need to have flexible hours or stick close to home. The advantages of telecommuting are many. You set your own schedule as to when you work. You eliminate your commuting time. It's a bit like being self-employed, except you are assured a paycheck at the end of the week, not to mention health benefits.

Is there a downside to telecommuting? Research shows that because telecommuters are out of sight, they tend to receive fewer promotions and get smaller raises. If you choose to work at home instead of in the office, it is important that you manage issues of visibility, perceived commitment, and communication.

Understand your organization's culture and how telecommuters are perceived. Bosses and organizations differ widely in their policies and practical approaches to supporting telecommuters. If your boss regularly telecommutes, then there are likely informal supports for the process. If neither your boss or colleagues telecommute, think carefully about what organizational norms you will break and how you will compensate for breaching them.

Take responsibility for communicating and maintaining your visibility. Even if your boss and organization support telecommuters, you will do well to communicate frequently. You will also need to expect a certain amount of face time (for example, to attend important meetings, marketing events, etc.).

Seek feedback to know if telecommuting is—or is not—working for you. When you start to telecommute, you should actively seek feedback from your boss and colleagues about how they perceive your working arrangement. Ask open-ended questions such as: "Since I often work at home, how am I doing in terms of communicating with you?" "Do you feel that I am easily accessible?" "Can you easily reach me when you want to?" These and similar questions open the door to honest conversations about how you might improve the situation.

Linking telecommuting to your employer's goals

Okay, you know why you are interested in working from home, but why should your boss be in favor of the arrangement? In other words, what's in it for your employer?

Telecommuting demands smart measures of employee productivity. The stereotypical image of old-style measures of employee "productivity" included such aspects as employees arriving early and staying late. In other words, the measures of "performance" were outward manifestations of "playing the game." In today's hypercompetitive global marketplace, such yardsticks of employee productivity are counterproductive.

Telecommuting, on the other hand, requires focusing on the work itself, rather than the trappings of a workplace. Calling a client in Japan at the client's convenience, for example, requires attention to the client's schedule rather than to a local 9-to-5 office routine. Telecommuting can, if structured to achieve individual and organizational goals, push employers to change and develop market-oriented measures of employee productivity.

Telecommuting can help retain talented employees. Research indicates that most people define a "great job" as one with freedom and autonomy to make decisions, a line of sight between daily activities and business results, challenging rather than overwhelming work, new projects on a frequent basis, and good relationships with colleagues. If managed with finesse, telecommuting places in the hands of employees decisions about when and where to work, the first definition of a "great job."

Resources for telecommuters

www.telecommute.org
The International Telework Association & Council is dedicated to promoting the benefits of telecommuting.

www.inteleworks.com
This site provides information for implementing a program.

www.telcom.org
This lobbying group promotes telecommuting with government officials.

www.iftf.org
The Web site of the Institute for the Future is a good resource on technology trends.

taking early retirement

Is it right for you?

If the thought of retiring from your career while you are still young enough to start a brand-new one appeals to you, then first thing you need to do is weigh the pros and cons. First, the most obvious challenge: money. A longer retirement means you'll have that many more years to support yourself without a full salary (unless, of course, you start a second career). You may also have to pay for your health insurance until Medicare kicks in at 65. On the plus side, retiring early can free you up to enjoy a more relaxed lifestyle or pursue hobbies and other interests. Early retirement calls for a lot of planning. Start by asking yourself:

Why do you want to retire early? What do you plan to do over the next 25 years? If you have no concrete plans other than not working, you may find yourself isolated and bored if you retire too soon and do not have a strong social network. On the other hand, if you're an active person, retiring early can free you up to volunteer, teach, travel, pursue your hobbies, or start a new career.

How long will you be retired? Today, the average life expectancy for thirtysomethings is 78 years (women) and 72 years (men). How many years would you be retired before reaching that age? This can help you find out how much you need to save.

How much will you need? At what rate will your retirement benefits pay? Will it be enough for you to enjoy the lifestyle you envision for your retirement? Like many Americans, you may not have financial resources to live for 30 years or more without working. So will you need to earn more first or make other investments to prepare for a longer retirement? There are online calculators (see Resources, page 193) that can help you figure out just how much you need to sock away and how much interest your savings will have to earn for you to live comfortably during your retirement. You can also consult a financial planner.

If everything looks good and retiring early seems plausible, start looking into retirement options at your company. Some companies—particularly after they merge or downsize—offer loyal, older employees a "golden handshake": a generous early-retirement package that often includes a one-time cash settlement.

Steps to retiring early

- Set goals and establish priorities regarding when you want to retire and how much you'll need

- Pay off any current liabilities, such as mortgages, credit card balances, and personal loans

- Make the maximum contribution you can to your 401(k) account

- Reduce expenses and build up your savings account

- Open an IRA (Individual Retirement Account) and contribute the maximum amount

- Determine your investment objectives with the help of a financial planner

Optional paths for older workers

Gradual retirement While some companies have mandatory retirement ages, there is no law that says you can't continue to work on a part-time basis or as a consultant.

Short-term projects with the old company Some companies are finding that retirees are an excellent labor pool for short-term or part-time work. These former employees understand the work environment and are efficient at their tasks. In addition, these older workers are trusted members of the organization's community.

Intermittent work Here senior professionals can sign up for various projects at their old company or at others. Consider signing on with a temporary executive placement firm that sends people out on three or four month-long projects. When the projects ends, you can either take time off or get another short-term assignment.

Self-employment Approximately 17 percent of workers 50 and over are self-employed, compared to 10 percent of the overall workforce. Older workers turn to self-employment for several reasons. Some are pushed into it, having lost their jobs, while others have severe health problems that constrain their work options. Yet another group of older Americans has the wealth and education to use self-employment as a transition into full retirement.

what do I do now?

I am a single woman in my 30s and I am an expert horseback rider. My boss encourages flexible schedules for the moms in the office, but I am expected to stay late to finish projects, missing my training appointments. This doesn't seem fair. How do I handle the situation?

Savvy bosses and organizations create work/life programs that are not gender specific and that recognize commitments in addition to those involving children.

Talk with your boss about the problem, directly addressing the issue of fairness. Perhaps redesigning workloads and tasks could eliminate the need for anyone to stay late. If, on the other hand, the nature of your business creates last-minute demands, discuss a rotational system with your boss, or offer to come in extra early to get work done. Since changing how people work takes preparation, thoughtful implementation, and steely determination, decide in advance how the office will monitor the results of any new plan.

I am thinking I might want to start my own business. How do I get started?

First, consider starting a business in your area of expertise and passion. Launch a business that you know lots about, and have the passion that will sustain you through the anxiety and uncertainty during start-up.

Start small Many people expand their hobbies or something they excel at.

Set realistic short- and long-term goals One work-from-home consultant who stepped off the fast track at a prestigious university put aside a year's salary before she struck out on her own. She sets quarterly and yearly goals for her earnings. Once she reaches her quarterly goals, she gives herself permission to accept new work or go to the beach.

Seek help as you get started There are countless books, courses, and Web sites that can help you get started, grow, and prosper. There are also countless scams claiming that you can make money through their opportunities. Be cautious.

I recently remarried. Both of us have teenage children from previous marriages. There is so much conflict among the kids and between my new spouse and myself over roles, relationships and household responsibilities that I cannot concentrate at work. How do I begin to sort through this mess?

Begin with your workplace's Employee Assistance Program to see what educational or professional resources might support you. There are classes on negotiation and conflict resolution that can be really helpful to teach you and your family members how to defuse family conflicts. As teenagers they are old enough to understand much of what is going on and to offer and implement suggestions for change. Learning how to de-escalate conflict and structure tasks to match the strengths of people are critical skills at home and at work.

Helpful Resources

WEB SITES

American Association of Retired People
www.aarp.org
The Web site for the American Association of Retired Persons is filled with information and resources about retirement. As the largest organization for older Americans, it also lobbies governments for policies and programs that benefit senior Americans.

MSN Money's Retirement Planner
http://moneycentral.msn.com/retire/planner.asp
Helps you figure out the amount you'll need to retire.

ResumeEdge.com
www.resumeedge.com
Advice for everyone from first-time job seekers to senior executives, including a résumé and cover letter editing service.

BOOKS

Mompreneurs: A Mother's Practical Step-by-Step Guide to Work-at-Home Success
by Patricia Cobe & Ellen H. Parlapiano

Work Naked: Eight Essential Principles for Peak Performance in the Virtual Workplace
by Cynthia Froggatt

The 12 BAD Habits that Hold GOOD People Back: Overcoming the Behavior Patterns that Keep You from Getting Ahead
by James Waldroop and Timothy Butler

Barnes & Noble Basics: Starting Your Own Business
by Joanne Cleaver

glossary

Affinity group

A group in an organization that is composed of people with some common characteristic (gender, job function, hobbies, sexual orientation, race) who come together to support and learn from one another.

Age Discrimination in Employment Act

Passed in 1978, this federal law prohibits employers from discriminating against people aged 40 and over. In some states, this age is as young as 18.

Ally

Someone who extends your sphere of influence by supporting your ideas and promoting them to others.

Americans with Disabilities Act

Passed in 1990, the ADA is a federal law that prohibits employers from discriminating against people based on their mental or physical disabilities, as long as those disabilities do not prevent those people from doing their jobs.

Aptitude and skill tests

These diagnostic tests determine how well you can perform a particular type of work. They may test your verbal reasoning (basic understanding of the written word), numerical reasoning (your basic math skills), or your analytical ability. Skills tests determine whether you can perform the job, while aptitude tests determine whether you can be trained to do the job in the future.

"At will"

The condition of working for an employer without a contract. By being employed "at will," you essentially can be fired at any time for any legal reason. On the flip side, it means you can quit at any time, too.

Benefits specialist

In an HR department, this is an expert in benefits (health, dental, life insurance, etc.) who helps employees understand the benefits offered by their organization.

Career integrator

A person who does not make clear distinctions between the three areas of his life (work, love, and play).

Career path

Conventionally a career path was a lifelong work trajectory that involved full-time work in one functional area, in which success was measured by a linear progression to the most senior position in the organization. In response to changing workplace dynamics, the definition of career path has expanded to include multiple paths, which can include full- or part-time work, taking time off, working successive jobs that don't necessarily build on one another, flextime jobs, or progressing along a nonlinear path in search of new challenges.

Career separator

A person who keeps clear boundaries between work, love, and play.

Civil Rights Act

Passed in 1964, this federal law prohibits employers from discriminating against people based on race, sex, national origin, ancestry, or religious beliefs.

Coaching

One-on-one instruction and guidance designed to improve your knowledge, skills, and work performance. Most often supervisors serve as coaches to improve the performance of their subordinates in specified areas.

Communication style

The unconscious rules a person follows when presenting and processing information. Style is shaped by factors like speed, the amount of detail and directness, and the amount of personal information imparted when communicating.

Compensation specialist

In an HR department, this is an expert in salaries and pay systems who helps employees understand the compensation system in their organization and in the industry at large.

Compressed workweek

A flexible work arrangement that allows employees to work a 40-hour workweek over less than five days.

Core competencies

The business activities that a company does best and that are essential for the survival of the enterprise. An example would be new product development at a research and development firm. Such activities are rarely outsourced and involvement in them is usually highly rewarded.

Counteroffer

An offer made by one side of a negotiating party in response to an offer made by the other side. An example would be when you receive a job offer from a prospective employer and, in an attempt to keep you from leaving, your current employer makes a counteroffer that includes a promotion or raise.

Culture

The system of underlying values and beliefs that guides the lives of the people in a community. In all cases, culture defines "the way we do it around here," and separates what is socially acceptable behavior from what is not. For example, arguing forcefully may be accepted in some workplaces, but not in others.

Decision-making style
The style a person uses when making a decision, which can include speed, type or number of facts involved, level of intuition used, the degree to which others are included, and the level of risk assumed by the decision-maker.

Defamation law
To prevent an employer from giving false information to a potential new employer, this law prevents him from speaking untruths ("slander") or writing untruths ("libel") about you.

Disagreement
A difference of opinion or perspective between people. It is critical to learn the unspoken rules for voicing disagreement in your organization if you want to be heard. It is also critical to prevent a disagreement from escalating into a conflict, in which another person feels personally attacked.

Discrimination
The act of being treated unfairly by an employer because you are a member of a protected group; e.g., to be denied a job based on your race.

Early adopter
A person who reads about, anticipates, and buys the latest technological gizmos on the market.

Eldercare
An employment benefit offered to employees who must care for aging parents; this often takes the form of referral services (helping them find care and support) or long-term care insurance (to protect savings during retirement).

Emotional intelligence
The kind of intelligence that allows you to control your impulses and emotions, anticipate and understand how you are perceived by others, and interpret and respond appropriately to others' feelings.

Employment contract
A detailed document that, in many companies, new employees have to sign before officially starting employment. It specifies what the company expects from you and what you can expect from the company in terms of performance, compensation, termination benefits, and more.

Executive coaching
The kind of career coaching that is provided to top-level employees, such as CEOs and VPs. More and more corporations are hiring executive coaches for their middle- and upper-level managers.

Executive search recruiter
An outside placement specialist hired on a fee or retainer basis by a company to screen job candidates for high-level positions. An executive search recruiter seeks job candidates among already-employed people with proven track records of success.

Exit interview
An interview that HR conducts with an employee who is leaving the company. The interview may include questions about the employee's reasons for leaving and his general experiences working for the company. Companies use this information to identify ways to improve their ability to attract and retain good employees.

Family and Medical Leave Act

This federal law requires that businesses with 50 or more employees provide 12 weeks of unpaid, job-guaranteed leave to employees who give birth to or adopt children. It also has provisions for employees who provide eldercare or care during a medical emergency.

Fit

One of the most influential but often unconscious factors in determining your attractiveness during job interviews and your ability to be successful once inside an organization. Fit is determined via the often implicit rules regarding how people work and interact within an organization.

Flextime

A flexible work arrangement in which employees organize a shorter workday around core business hours; e.g., 10 a.m. to 3 p.m.

Gendered expectations

Societal rules that specify how men are expected to behave one way and women another. When interacting, each gender expects the other to follow those rules. These rules may be unspoken but are nevertheless taught and reinforced through the media, literature, platitudes, folklore, religion, etc.

Group mentoring

When several people of approximately the same level of experience and job responsibilities come together as a collective to give one another career advice and emotional support.

Hypercompetitive

This describes the state of the world marketplace, in which many people from large and small, rich and poor countries are chasing similar products and economic goals.

Hypernetworking

The practice of taking personal networking online, which allows people to expand their connections exponentially.

Immigration Reform and Control Act

Passed in 1986, this federal law prohibits discrimination against legal aliens based on their national origin or citizenship status.

Interest inventory

A diagnostic test that measures your preferences in a broad range of occupations, leisure activities, and subjects.

Jobless recovery

The phenomenon that occurred in the early 2000s, in which the economy turned around and resulted in employers increasing their spending and investing levels, but not their hiring levels.

Job-sharing program

A flexible work arrangement in which two people share a single full-time position.

Letter of recommendation

A letter that you may ask Human Resources or your boss to write for you that gives the start and end dates of your employment, your job title(s), and a list of your responsibilities. Because of legal constraints, these letters rarely comment on the quality of your work.

Letter of resignation

A letter, sometimes required by the organization, that you write upon leaving a position and that spells out the date of your departure. In the letter you may also explain why you are leaving, but if you do, it is a good strategy to keep the letter positive and nonaccusatory.

Lifelong learning

The strategy of engaging in structured and challenging educational activities throughout your life.

Management buyout

In this method for reducing the size of a company's workforce, employees are offered generous severance packages in exchange for leaving willingly. Usually it is wise to take the buyout, as the offer probably indicates financial distress that may later result in forced layoffs.

Mentor

A successful, higher-level employee who shares her experience, knowledge, and emotional support with someone less experienced. A mentor can help you further your career by teaching you how to be successful in an organization and by giving you objective feedback. A mentor can be formally assigned by an organization; more often, the relationship is formed informally between two people who have similar values and appreciate each other.

Mentoring circle

A formally recognized group of coworkers that meets regularly with a senior leader, who provides career advice and support.

Negotiations

The back-and-forth, give-and-take process that a new hire and an employer engage in when trying to come to an agreement over the terms of a job (salary, benefits, etc.). Usually, the parties have dissimilar interests and must find compromises that suit both of them.

Network

The personal and professional relationships you form with people who know what you do and know your career goals. These people are invaluable sources of information and can connect you with people who are hiring. You are also part of their networks and, as such, should provide them information and connections to others.

Noncompete or nonsolicitation agreement

A promise that you make (when signing an employment contract or accepting a severance package) that you will not set up a company that directly competes with the company you are joining or leaving, and that you will not contact any of your current employer's clients.

Norms

These are the explicit or implicit rules for behavior inside any work group that guide what people do. Norms ensure that employees' behaviors exemplify a community's underlying values.

Office politics

Most broadly, these are the strategies and tactics coworkers use to compete for scarce resources in an organization. Relationships are created and maintained in an effort to get the support, visibility, funding, and access needed to meet organizational and personal goals.

Offshore outsourcing, or offshoring

The practice of sending work to other countries to take advantage of lower labor costs. While this has long been occurring in manufacturing, beginning in the early 2000s it expanded to also include many jobs that involve voice or data technologies.

"Old boys' network"

The often invisible network of support and resources provided by men to other men in an organization. This support is not usually extended to women or people of color.

Outplacement services

These services are provided by internal HR staff or a hired outside firm to support those who have been laid-off and are looking for a new job. Services may include help with writing résumés, practice interviews, diagnostic testing, and career advice.

Outsourcing

The practice of allocating work to another company that manages every aspect of a set of tasks. In the 1980s, companies began outsourcing non-core work such as food service, maintenance, and even technology. Outsourcing can be a threat to you (can your job be outsourced?) or an opportunity (can you be a contract worker?).

Peer mentor

Someone who has approximately the same level of experience, status, and job responsibilities as you, and with whom you share career strategies and support in a mentoring relationship.

Personal board of directors

A group of people you select who are dedicated to your career success and provide career advice, objective feedback, insights, and contacts.

Personality test

A diagnostic instrument that reveals aspects of your personality and then correlates them to the type of work that people with your personality profile find satisfying.

Politically savvy

This describes someone who recognizes the power dynamics inherent in work relationships and conducts herself in such a manner that she stays on the positive side of an organization's powerful people.

Pregnancy Discrimination Act

Passed in 1978, this federal law prohibits discrimination in hiring or promoting pregnant women, or women with pregnancy-related medical conditions.

Professional association

A fee-for-membership group in which people of a particular profession come together to develop their job-related skill sets and organize conferences and educational programs to make career-enhancing connections between its members.

Profile statement

Often at the top of a résumé, this is two or three sentences that catch the reader's attention by describing what you offer to the potential employer. The statement may include your key skills and strengths and a summary of your work experience.

Protected class

A group of people protected by state or federal law that prohibits discrimination on the basis of age, race, sex, national origin, ancestry, religion, or physical or mental disabilities.

Qualifiers

Words such as "maybe," "possibly," "a little," which dilute the impact of your comments. Avoiding such words in an interview or presentation will make you sound more confident and competent.

Résumé

A one- or two-page document that describes your educational and professional experience. It can also include a mission statement, as well as a list of awards, professional association memberships, and specific skills.

Rule of reciprocity
The idea that, over time, people expect to be paid back for what they do. People who are always taking and never giving in an office are often called freeloaders for not pulling their weight. This label can dramatically diminish your ability to influence others, get work done, or get promoted.

Severance pay
A monetary settlement based on the number of years you were employed with an organization. Most companies have a standard formula for determining this, but it still is negotiable.

Severance or separation package
A closing settlement between you and your employer regarding what they owe you and what you owe them. This may include the numbers of days you have to work before leaving, the benefits owed you, an agreement to provide outplacement services, an arrangement to let you purchase your company computer, etc.

Sexual dynamics
The normal force of physical attraction that can occur between people in the workplace.

Sexual harassment
State and federal laws define this as unwanted sexual advances or visual, verbal, or physical conduct of a sexual nature that interferes with your ability to do your job.

Social identity
The identity that society bestows upon you that is delineated by your race, age, gender, cultural background, physical abilities, sexual orientation, and other characteristics.

Specialization
The process of acquiring and using knowledge in a particular area or developing a deep expertise in one area (rather than across many).

Sponsor
Someone who uses his influence and power in an organization to advance your career. He might suggest your name for a vacated position or present a positive explanation and support you when your actions are questioned.

Step-ahead mentor
A mentor who is one rung up the organizational ladder from her protégé.

Subsidized child care
An employment benefit in which child-care payments are made on a sliding scale, with the company paying a larger proportion for lower-salary employees.

Success stories
Two-minute stories about past accomplishments that you use throughout an interview to illustrate your skills and competencies. Each story should include a concise description of a problem, challenge, or opportunity you faced in the past, what you did about it, and what the positive, measurable outcome was.

Succession planning
A program in some companies whereby top employees are groomed and mentored so that they can eventually move up into higher positions as those jobs are vacated, ensuring the company's ongoing stability and success.

Telecommuting

A flexible work arrangement in which employees are based at home and connect to the office via the Internet.

Trailblazer

Someone who is the only employee (or one of only a few employees) of a particular social identity or background. Because of this unique role, a trailblazer must face up to expectations about how she is "supposed" to behave and succeed in the workplace.

Training specialist

In an HR department, this is an expert in administering the company's sponsored training programs, such as computer software classes or time-management classes. See *Benefits*

Tween support

An employment benefit in which child care is provided for children ages 5 to 12, often in the form of on-site care, after-school programs, or camp programs for children who are too young to stay at home alone but too old for traditional day care.

Unjust dismissal law

There is no federal law protecting you against unjust dismissal from a job, but each state does have a law on this; however, each law defines "unjust dismissal" differently, giving most employees little to stand on.

Visibility

An essential aspect of career success, this means not just doing good work, but the quality of making your work visible to the people who have the power to influence your career progression.

Vision statement

A two- or three-sentence statement that defines what you want for your career. It may include specific or broad language about the type of work you want to do, the level of authority you want, and the type of organization you want to work for.

Whistle-blower

An employee who reports a company's or coworker's illegal or wrongful activities to state or federal authorities, often at the cost of his job and career.

Work style

The unique way in which a person approaches a work task. A person's work style can be shaped by the speed with which he completes a task, his level of involvement with other people, the time of day when his energy is highest, how much he procrastinates, and the amount of structure and order he prefers to have when working.

index

A

affinity groups, 28, 37, 39, 194
Age Discrimination in Employment
    Act (1978), 49, 194
age issues, 36, 49, 194
alliances, forming, 123
alumni groups, 28
Americans with Disabilities Act
    (1990), 49, 194
associations
    as career-enhancing connection,
        126–127
    professional, 126–127, 150, 199
    recognition by, 126–127
    selecting, 126–127
attire, 41
    sexually provocative, 46

B

backstabbing, 78
bargaining, 76
behavior, analyzing one's own, 98
benefits specialists, 26, 195
biculturalism, 43
books
    *Barnes & Noble Basics: Résumés
        and Cover Letters*, 175
    *Barnes & Noble Basics: Starting
        Your Own Business*, 193
    *Barnes & Noble Basics: Your Job
        Interview*, 175
    Beyond Performance, 73
    *Breaking Through: The Making of
        Minority Executives in Corporate
        America*, 53
    Career Bounce Back!, 175
    The Career Survival Guide, 95
    *Career Warfare: 10 Rules for
        Building a Successful Personal
        Brand and Fighting to Keep It*,
        29
    Difficult Conversations, 95

Disappearing Acts, 53
Do's and Taboos Around the World,
    53
Emotional Intelligence, 113
*The Empowered Manager: Positive
    Political Skills at Work*, 151
*The Etiquette Advantage in
    Business: Personal Skills for
    Professional Success*, 95
Everyday Negotiation, 151
Firing Back, 175
*The Five Patterns of Extraordinary
    Careers: The Guide for Achieving
    Success and Satisfaction*, 131
Getting to the Top, 53
*Global Trends 2005: An Owner's
    Manual for the Next Decade*, 29
How to Shine at Work, 73, 175
Influence Without Authority, 95
*Leading in Black and White:
    Working Across the Racial
    Divide in Corporate America*, 53
*The Lessons of Experience: How
    Successful Executives Develop on
    the Job*, 151
*Mompreneurs: A Mother's Practical
    Step-by-Step Guide to Work-at-
    Home Success*, 193
Never Wrestle with a Pig, 73
*Nice Girls Don't Get the Corner
    Office: 101 Unconscious Mistakes
    Women Make That Sabotage
    Their Careers*, 113, 151
*Our Separate Ways: Black and
    White Women and the Struggle
    for Professional Identity*, 53
The Platinum Rule, 95
*The Practical Coach: Management
    Skills for Everyday Life*, 29, 131
*The Shadow Negotiation: How
    Women Can Master the Hidden
    Agendas that Determine*

Bargaining Success, 151
*The Smart Woman's Guide to
    Career Success*, 131
Talking from 9 to 5, 53
*Trendspotting: Think Forward, Get
    Ahead, and Cash in on the
    Future*, 29
*The 12 BAD Habits that Hold
    GOOD People Back: Overcoming
    the Behavior Patterns that Keep
    You from Getting Ahead*, 193
*Working with Emotional
    Intelligence*, 113
*Work Naked: Eight Essential
    Principles for Peak Performance
    in the Virtual Workplace*, 193
You Just Don't Understand, 53
bosses
    apprising of progress, 59
    becoming irreplaceable to, 62–63
    communication style, 56
    decision-making styles, 56
    difficult, 66–67
    getting along with, 62–63
    getting feedback from, 59, 82–83
    getting to know, 56–57
    informing of other job openings,
        145
    loyalty to, 59
    managing, 58–59
    as partners, 58
    priorities of, 61
    problem, 64–67
    relationship with, 58–59
    skills of, 56
    understanding, 60–61
    work styles, 56

C

career
    alternative paths, 182–183
    balancing life and, 178–193

changing, 168
coaching, 24–25
deciding to move on, 166–167
defining, 9
development, 10–11
issue of fit, 44–45
flexible arrangements, 186–187
gamesmanship quality, 101
goals, 14–15
handling emotion in, 101
importance of allies in, 116–117
inappropriate communications in 101
integrators, 180
internal promotion, 134–135
managing, 8
market changes and, 22–23
mistakes, 100–101
moving to new company, 154–175
moving up in, 134–151
need for understanding the culture of an organization, 101
overturning roadblocks in, 98–113
paths, 195
personal review of, 13
portfolio, 12–13
project work, 136–137
recognizing need for change in, 101
recruiters and, 160–161
reviving, 164–165
separators, 180
short-term challenges to, 184–185
skill building, 16
specialties, 17
specializing, 18–19
stalled, 164–165
taking stock, 154–155
trajectory, 8
traps, 165
values and, 179
vision statement, 12
change
  imperative to, 110
  agents, 11
  aging of baby boomers, 23
  career, 168
  communicating reasons for, 111
  in companies, 9

in demographics, 22–23, 53
diversity and, 23
loyalty and, 111
market, 22–23
organizational, 9
recognition of need for, 101
resistance to, 110
support for, 110
taking advantage of, 18
in women's participation in work force, 23, 53
child care, 187
Civil Rights Act (1964), 49, 195
coaching, 24–25, 195
  executive, 196
coalitions, 76
colleagues
  affiliations and, 85
  dating, 46
  disagreeing with, 90–91
  establishing respect with, 87
  finding common ground with, 45
  getting feedback from, 82–83
  handling differences with, 86–87
  managing conflict with, 92–93
  negotiating with, 88–89
  office politics and, 76–79
  peer mentoring and, 121
  problem, types of 80–81
  pulling one's weight with, 84–85
  rapport with, 122
  relationships with, 10, 76–81
  respect for, 122
  trust in, 122
communication
  e-mail, 108–109
  instant messaging (IM), 109
  language used, 104–105
  blunders, 104–105
  and reasons for changes, 111
  styles, 195
  technical jargon in, 104
  tone of voice in, 104, 109
  written, 106
compensation specialists, 26, 195
competition, 22
  for resources, 76
computers. *See also* telecommuting

literacy in, 16
software, 21
online research, 163
conference attendance, 57
conflict
  avoiding, 77
  handling, 35
  management, 92–93
  office politics and, 77
  resolution, 44
corporate culture, 10, 34–35
  conflict handling in, 35
  decision making and, 35
  gendered expectations and promotion in, 146–147
  information sharing in, 35
  norms for behavior and, 34
  playing by the rules in, 34, 44, 52
  in meetings, 99
  relationships in, 35
  social interaction in, 35
  understanding, 35
cultural
  collisions, 42
  differences, 40
  identity, 41
  knowledge, 38
  norms, 42
  sensitivity, 38, 40
  slang, 41
  symbols, 43
culture
  dominant, fitting into, 41
  mainstream, 42–43

D

decision making, 35
  by bosses, 56
  at meetings, 99
  styles, 196
demographics, 22–23, 53
demotions, 73
development
  career, 38
  flexibility in, 11
  market changes and, 22–23
  in mentoring relationships, 119

ongoing, 10–11
plans, 10
product, 39
professional, 126–127
programs, 26
differences
with colleagues, 86–87
cultural, 40
survival strategies, 47
diplomacy, 90–91
disabilities, 36, 50–51
accommodations for, 50
stereotypes and, 50
discrimination, 196
age, 194
dealing with, 48–49
legal action and, 48
protections, 48
sexual politics and, 46
survival strategies, 47
diversity
addressing, 36–37
appreciation of, 92
awareness, 38
bridging differences, 45
career effects of, 23
celebrating, 38–39
cross-cultural concerns, 40–41
hidden expectations on, 147
investigating, 37
in management, 43
as market force, 36
productivity and, 38–39
programs, 36
role of, 45
social identities and, 36
stereotypes and, 36
support for, 38
documentation
career highlights, 12
quarterly statements, 13
downsizing, 156–157
Drucker, Peter, 14
dynamics, sexual, 46
definition of, 47

E

education

community resources, 19
continuous process of, 10
to update skills, 20
e-mail, 52–53, 108–109
attachments to, 109
distribution of, 108
formatting, 109
privacy issues, 109
replying to, 108
Employee Assistance Program (EAP),
184
employment
"at will," 194
child care and, 187
flexible arrangements, 186
job-sharing, 186
overseas, 11
part-time, 186
project-based, 11
self, 191
experience
international, 11
need for, 11

F

Family and Medical Leave Act,
184–185, 196
feedback
from boss, 71
from colleagues, 155
collective, 98
mistakes and, 103
negative, 98
360-degree, 98
flexibility, 11
dealing with change and, 18
flextime, 186, 197

G

gender, 36
expectations, 47
promotion and, 146–147
globalization, 22
goals
attaining, 15–17
backup plans for, 15
checking progress, 15
company, 12

elimination of barriers to, 15
flexibility in reaching, 15
long-term, 14
measuring progress in attaining,
14–15
"must have," 14–15
quota, 12
realistic, 10
setting, 10, 14–15
short-term, 14
gossip, 78, 81

H

harassment, sexual, 46–47, 200
hierarchies, 99
hobby clubs, 28
human resources
benefits specialists, 26
recruitment, 26
reward systems in, 26
ties with, 26–27
training/development programs, 26
humor, 102
hypernetworking, 131, 197

I

Immigration Reform and Control Act
(1986), 49, 197
information
computer, 21
from networks, 124
for promotion purposes, 134
sharing, 35, 45
technological, 21
instant messaging (IM), 109
insurance
health, 26
long-term care, 185
interaction
with majority group, 45
new forms of, 20
social, 35
Internet. See also Web sites
educational courses on, 20
need for familiarity with, 20
pace of business and, 22
interviewing, 169
in another department, 144–145

J

job-sharing programs, 186
jokes
    sexist, 52, 79
    racist, 79

K

knowledge, specialized, 17–19

L

language, 104–105
    foreign, 11, 16
    skills, 31
    slang, 104
    standard English, 41
    technical jargon, 104
    weak, 105
layoffs, 157
learning
    lifelong, 10
    what's valued in one's industry, 18
legislation
    Age Discrimination in Employment
        Act (1978), 49, 194
    Americans with Disabilities Act
        (1990), 49, 194
    Civil Rights Act (1964), 49, 195
    discrimination, 49
    Immigration Reform and Control
        Act (1986), 49, 197
    Pregnancy Discrimination Act
        (1978), 49, 199
loyalty, 111

M

management
    of bosses, 58, 59
    buyouts, 167, 198
    diversity in, 43
    skills, 16
marketing oneself, 68–69
meetings
    career-building behavior during, 99
    handling unexpected situations, 99
    seating hierarchies, 99
memos, 107
mentors/mentoring, 36, 38, 43
    in career promotions, 116–117

choosing, 43, 47
circles, 121, 198
formal, 118–119
functions of, 118
group, 120–121, 197
peer, 121, 199
qualities to look for in, 117
rule of reciprocity in, 120
step-ahead, 119–200
minorities. *See also* diversity
    recruitment, 37
mistakes
    in communication, 104–105
    feedback and, 103
    informing boss of, 102
    taking responsibility for, 102–103
motivation, 45

N

negotiation, 198
    for promotion, 142–143
    responses to, 89
    salary, 88–89
    skills, 16, 143
networks, 198
    alumni, 129
    assessing, 124–125
    caring for, 128–129
    charity work and, 129
    depth of, 124
    educational, 129
    expanding, 124
    groups, 36, 39
    informal support, 28–29
    information from, 124
    keeping track of, 128
    of mentors, 10
    multidimensional, 128
    "old boys," 198
    online, 130–131
    outside work, 129
    professional associations, 126–127
    reciprocity in, 128
    social, 129
    sports and, 129
    support, 10
nonfraternization policy, 46
norms, 198

corporate, 34
cultural, 42
reconciling differences, 42, 43
understanding, 35

O

office politics, 76–77, 198
offshoring, 22
organizations
    becoming indispensable to, 22
    change in, 9, 11, 110–111
    financial health of, 156
    layoffs in, 157
    matching personal values to,
        43, 44, 45
    need for understanding culture of,
        101
    researching, 158, 162–163
    staffing levels in, 9
outsourcing, 22, 198, 199

P

performance
    appraisals, 139
    publicizing, 68–69
    reviews, 70, 71
    salary increases and, 139
Peters, Tom, 28
politics
    backstabbing and, 78
    being passed over, 79
    colleagues and, 76–81
    false rumors and, 78
    gossip and, 78
    office, 76–77, 198
    sexual, 46–47
    types of, 78, 79
    unethical behavior, 79
Popcorn, Faith, 175
portfolio
    building, 12–13
    documentation in, 12
Pregnancy Discrimination Act (1978),
    49, 199
presentations, 105
privacy issues
    in e-mails, 109
    in instant messages, 110

in online networks, 131
programs
    career development, 38
    development, 26
    diagnostic, 98
    diversity, 36
    eldercare, 185
    income protection, 185
    job-sharing, 186, 197
    maternity leave, 185
    mentoring, 36
    professional development, 126–127
    retirement, 26
    training, 19, 24–26
project-based employment, 11
projects
    becoming involved with, 136–137
    as career opportunities, 136–137
    delegating tasks within, 137
promotion, 68–69, 111, 134–151
    asking for, 140–141
    being noticed for, 135
    choosing right time to request, 140
    deciding on, 148–149
    gendered expectations in, 146–147
    hidden expectations in, 147
    internal opportunities, 134–135
    interviewing in another
        department, 144–145
    marketing oneself for, 134
    need for information about, 134
    negotiating for, 142–143
    obtaining raises, 138–139
    preparation for, 141
    recruiters and, 160–161
    tips, 135
    using S-T-A-R-T success stories, 141

R
race, 36
    jokes and, 79
raises. See also promotion
    asking for, 138
    earning, 138–139
rapport in relationships, 122
reciprocity
    in networking, 128
    in relationships, 122, 128

recruiters, 26, 160–161
recruitment, minority, 37
relationships
    adversarial, 58
    alliances, 123
    with bosses, 56, 57
    building, 116–131
    caring for, 128
    with colleagues, 10, 76–81
    with former colleagues, 28
    growth of, 116
    maintaining while telecommuting,
        95
    mentoring, 116–119
    productive working, 122–123
    rapport in, 122
    reciprocity in, 10, 122, 128
    respect and, 122
    strategic, 116–131
    structure of, 35
    trust and, 122
    virtual, 20
    working, 122–123
reliability, 62
relocation, 161
resignation, 166–173, 197
resources. See books; Web sites
respect
    establishing, 87
    in relationships, 122
résumés, 159
    use of value-adding projects, 11
retirement
    early, 190–191
    gradual, 191
    programs, 26
    short-term projects and, 191
reviews, performance, 70–71
roadblocks, 98–113
rumors, 78

S
salary
    cost-of-living and, 138
    negotiating for, 88–89
    obtaining raises in, 138–139
    options, 88
self-awareness, 10

self-promotion, 68–69
sensitivity, 101
sexual
    dynamics, 46, 200
    harassment, 46–47, 200
    jokes, 79
    orientation, 36
    politics, 46–47
    provocation, 46
skills
    of bosses, 56
    building, 19
    coping, 44
    foreign language, 16
    gaps in, 19
    interview, 56
    language, 31
    levels of, 19
    management, 16
    negotiation, 16, 143
    speaking, 16
    specialized, 17–19
    technology, 20–21
    tests, 194
    transferable, 168
    updating, 20
    writing, 16, 106–107
slang, 104
social
    identity, 36, 42, 200
    interaction, 35
    needs, 44
    networks, 129
speaking, public, 16, 19
specialization, 17–19, 22
sponsors, 47
S-T-A-R-T success stories, 141
succession planning, 38
support
    child care,187
    from coaches, 24–25
    from mentors, 118–119
    from mentoring groups, 120–121
    informal, 28–29
    tween, 187
    from Employee Assistance Program
        (EAP), 184
swearing, 104